NOTTINGHAMSHI

MURDEI
CASEBOOK

NOTTINGHAMSHIRE

MURDER
CASEBOOK

DAVID BELL

COUNTRYSIDE BOOKS
NEWBURY · BERKSHIRE

First published 1997
© David Bell 1997

COUNTRYSIDE BOOKS
3 Catherine Road
Newbury, Berkshire

ISBN 1 85306 476 9

Produced through MRM Associates Ltd., Reading
Typeset by Techniset Typesetters, Newton-le-Willows
Printed by J. W. Arrowsmith Ltd., Bristol

For Joan Bell

a mother, grandmother, great-grandmother,
a good friend to all who know her,
a Melton character since 1915,
and – at the age of 80 – a one-hour aeroplane pilot.

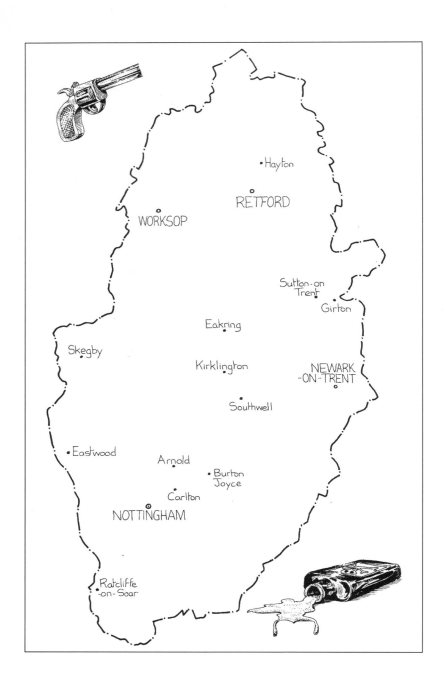

CONTENTS

ACKNOWLEDGEMENTS

I would like to express my thanks for their help and co-operation to the staff of Nottinghamshire Local Studies Library, and to the editors and staff of the *Nottingham Post*, the *Newark Advertiser* and the *Wolverhampton Express & Star*. I am also grateful for individual help generously given to me by Peter N. Walker, Peter Goodman, George Jackson, John Sutton, John Picket, Paul Fowldes, John Brunton, Mark Green, Frances Cartwright and John West.

INTRODUCTION

The idea of a Nottinghamshire Constabulary was first mooted at a meeting of the quarter sessions held in Southwell in October 1839. A special committee of magistrates – including the Duke of Portland and the Earl of Lincoln – was set up to look into the concept. This committee recommended that a Chief Constable should be appointed, on an annual salary of £250, with a force of eight superintendents and 33 constables under his command. The superintendents were to receive £75 per annum, and the constables 16 shillings per week. A later meeting of the quarter sessions approved this expenditure, and even upgraded the Chief Constable's salary to £300 per annum, and the constables' wages to 18 shillings a week; the salaries of the superintendents, however, were to remain at the recommended figure.

The county force was inaugurated in 1840, five years after the city of Nottingham had organised its constabulary into a regular force. The city continued to have its own force, as did the towns of Newark and Retford. Retford's police force, established in 1835, remained separate for only six years, coming into the county force in 1841. However, the independent Newark Borough force – which by the outbreak of World War II consisted of a Chief Constable, one inspector, four sergeants and 21 constables – joined the Nottinghamshire Constabulary in 1947, the Newark Chief Constable, R. T. Millhouse, opting to become a superintendent in the county force. The present Nottinghamshire Constabulary was formed in 1968, when the final amalgamation, that of the county and Nottingham city police forces, took place.

One of the more controversial Chief Constables of the Nottingham City force was Captain Athelstan Popkess, whose period in office ran from 1930 to 1960. Captain Popkess was born

9

in South Africa and became a professional soldier in that country. His army service with the notorious Black and Tans in Ireland in the 1920s, plus his lack of police force experience, led some members of the city council to oppose his selection for the post in 1930, but his appointment was upheld by the Home Secretary. Captain Popkess was then 37 years of age, the youngest holder of the office of Chief Constable in the country. He was a firm believer that all police officers should be big, strong and fit, and his force of 625 men had an average height of six feet two-and-a-half inches. Captain Popkess encouraged his men to take up boxing, and he always accompanied the Nottingham police boxing team to the Stuttgart area of Germany in the late 1930s. His close friend, Adolph Klaiber, the Stuttgart Police Chief, was made honorary president of the Nottingham Police Athletic Club, and during visits of the German police boxing team, the Swastika actually flew side by side with the Union Jack in Nottingham!

In 1959, Captain Popkess brought in officers from Scotland Yard to investigate alleged irregularities by certain members of the city council who had visited East Germany. He refused to give any information about the nature of these 'irregularities' to his Watch Committee, and he was therefore suspended from duty. His uncompromising battles with the city council split the population of Nottingham into two opposing camps, with his supporters – known as the Nottingham Vigilantes – taking to the streets. The Watch Committee reluctantly reinstated him in August 1959, at the insistence of the Home Secretary. Captain Popkess resigned a few months later and left Nottingham.

Although regarded as a reactionary figure in many ways, Athelstan Popkess was a forward-looking pioneer in several areas of police work. He was the first Chief Constable to introduce two-way radios for his officers, the first to have a forensic science laboratory, and the first to introduce police cadets. His ideas on the use of police dogs, traffic wardens and breathalysers were thought to be extremely radical at the time he suggested them; all three are now accepted as normal and helpful adjuncts to everyday police work. He died in Torquay in 1967, a year before the city force merged with that of the county.

The first Chief Constable of the new combined police force was John Browne, who had been head of the former county force since 1949. He retired in 1970, and was succeeded by Rex

Fletcher (1970–6), then by Charles MacLachlan (1976–82).

In 1979, Sherwood Lodge in Arnold, Nottingham, was opened as the new police headquarters, and the former HQ, Epperson Manor, became the force training school.

Nottingham City Police had a woman police constable in 1919, but the first women to serve in the county force were appointed in 1946. Until the combined force was created in 1968, the county police had only one female police inspector, Doris M. Carr. Cadets were first used by the county police in 1951, when 29 were appointed. These were all young men aged between 16 and 18; the first women cadets were recruited in 1966. One cadet who joined in 1974 was PC Christopher Dean, who later found international fame through his ice-dancing partnership with Jayne Torvill.

1

A
STRIKING WOMAN

The Murder of Joseph Barber at Eastwood
1851

Joseph Barber was a horse-dealer and a rogue, well known in the village of Eastwood. He was also one for the ladies, bragging that there wasn't a good-looking woman in Eastwood he hadn't bedded, adding with a roll of his eyes that he'd had quite a few of the plain ones too, if the nights were dark enough. Joe was 28, but one village girl he had his eye on was 15 year old Sarah.

Sarah was a striking girl; she was six feet two inches tall, with a good figure, fair hair and an attractive face. She was an orphan, her father having died before her birth, and her mother when she was two. Her grandmother had brought her up, and had recently died, leaving her £1,000. It may have been the sight of a handsome girl he hadn't yet seduced, or possibly the thought of her legacy, but Joe Barber decided to set his sights on tall young Sarah. Despite his rascally ways, Joe could be a charmer when he wanted, and he soon managed to have his wicked way with the girl. However, on this occasion he decided to make an honest woman of her, and married her two years later.

The marriage was not a happy one. He would often hit her when he was drunk, and on one occasion chased her down the street, beating her with a stick. Sarah's money was soon spent, and Joe Barber went back to his lecherous womanising. However, Sarah was a woman of strong character, not easily intimidated. After three years of marriage, she left her husband and went to live in Paris with a man called Gillot. When this lover turned out to be a replica of her husband, she threw him out and continued to live in Paris on her own.

Suddenly, Joe Barber reappeared in her life. He turned up at her home, begging her to return to him. He claimed that he was now a reformed character and had given up drinking and chasing women. Like many a woman before her, Sarah believed that her husband was genuinely repentant, that he was a leopard with changed spots! Perhaps he was, for a while, but he soon slipped back into his former habits.

However, Joe did not have things all his own way. Sarah was now as strong mentally as she was physically. When he thought he could use his fists on her, she handed him a good dose of his own medicine. It was really quite amusing: Joe Barber was feared by most of the men of the village, but at home . . . he had met his match.

The couple actually stayed together, but Joe's health began to deteriorate. He suffered from gonorrhoea – a souvenir of his lifestyle – and rheumatic fever left him an invalid. The life of Joe and Sarah became more peaceful. She nursed him well and he was grateful. When the nursing became too much for her, Joe took in a lodger, a young shoemaker called Robert Ingram. In return for his lodgings, Robert helped to nurse the ailing Joe Barber. In March 1851 Joe made a will, leaving the house and three acres of land to his wife. Although the land was mortgaged, it would provide a steady income for Sarah. Joseph's condition seemed very variable at this time. One day he would appear very weak indeed, the next he would be well enough to go to the pub with Rob Ingram or for a walk with Sarah. But after a few months, he was so ill that Sarah sent for his mother; soon afterwards Joe died.

Then the gossiping began. Remembering the fights and rows that Joe and Sarah used to have, people started saying that maybe she wanted him dead. Putting together the recent will in her favour, and the fact that there was a young man lodging at her house, malicious tongues passed on salacious rumours. Perhaps Robert and Sarah had conspired to poison Joe Barber.

A post-mortem was held, and arsenic was found in the dead man's liver. Sarah Barber and Robert Ingram were arrested and put on trial for murder. The prosecution made much of the fact that only Sarah or Robert had the opportunity to administer the poison; the defence pointed out that the evidence was both slight and circumstantial. When the verdict came in, Robert was found innocent and Sarah guilty. The judge ordered Ingram to be released, then he donned his black cap and sentenced Sarah Barber to hang. Drawing herself up to her full and magnificent height, Sarah told the court, 'Gentlemen of the jury, if you have found me guilty in this world, you cannot find me guilty in the next. Gentlemen, I am not guilty. I am as innocent as a child just born.' Sarah then shocked the court by walking over to Robert Ingram and kissing him warmly on the lips. It seems likely that the court drew their own conclusions about this show of passion, which appeared to confirm their verdict: the pair were lovers and she had wanted her husband dead.

In Nottingham Gaol, awaiting her execution, Sarah demanded to see the prison governor, Mr Hillyard, together with a magistrate. She swore a statement before them, saying that after her husband's death Robert Ingram had admitted his guilt. He told Sarah that he had bought some arsenic on the Sunday, and mixed it with Joseph's medicine. Sarah had administered the medicine to her husband in good faith, unaware that it contained poison.

The magistrate and the prison governor were inclined to treat Sarah's statement as the last attempt of a condemned woman to avoid her execution. Nevertheless, the governor came back to Sarah two days later, and asked her if she could prove what she had sworn. She told him that the medicine bottle which had contained the poisoned medicine was in the wash-house; she also recommended that they talk to Robert Ingram because she still believed him to be a truthful man.

Mr Hillyard acted on what he had been told, and the medicine bottle containing traces of arsenic was found where Sarah had said. When Ingram was questioned, he admitted that Sarah had spoken the truth: he had indeed poisoned Joseph Barber without Sarah's knowledge. This placed the authorities in an anomalous position. The man now admitting the murder had already been tried and found not guilty. He could not be tried again for the same crime. Eventually, Robert Ingram faced the lesser charge of felony, and received a short prison sentence.

Sarah Barber was not released, despite Ingram having confirmed her innocence. The death sentence was revoked and she was transported to Australia. She put her ill-starred life in

Eastwood behind her, served out her time, then married again, making a more careful choice of partner this time. In Australia, this strong and resourceful woman carved out a new and happy life for herself.

2

PRACTICE
MAKES PERFECT

The Murders of William Onions and Henry Westby Sr
in Nottingham

1881

Although Henry Westby Jr was of above average intelligence, his behaviour was eccentric to the point of being bizarre. In the Nottingham solicitors' office where he worked as a clerk, he insisted on working behind a screen, believing that the other clerks were continuously 'looking at him'. He also developed a hatred for his father, whom he accused of continually finding fault with him. This hatred grew so strong that the 18 year old youth decided his father would have to die. The only factor that gave him any doubts about his resolve to commit patricide was the nagging doubt over whether he would have the strength of mind to go through with the action. He decided therefore, with paranoid logic, that he would need to practise on someone else before murdering his father.

Returning one evening to the Wheelergate offices of Fraser's, where he worked, he noted that the only other person on the premises was William Onions, the 14 year old office boy. Carrying an iron bar, Henry crept up behind the boy and smashed him over the head with it. William fell to the floor, and Henry Westby slashed at his face and neck with a large knife until the boy was dead. As he observed the dead boy lying in a pool of blood, Henry felt no remorse, only an overwhelming satisfaction that he had proved himself capable of murder. The practising was over; he could now go through with the real thing.

Leaving the corpse of his young colleague lying on the office floor, Henry went out and made his vital purchase – a revolver – and then walked home to the tobacconist's shop off St Ann's Well Road where he lived with his parents. At 10 o'clock, he said goodnight to them and went up to bed, and an hour later Mr and Mrs Westby also retired to their bed.

At about 2.30 am, Mr Westby heard a noise downstairs and thought the shop was being burgled. He went downstairs only to be met by his son, who coolly levelled the revolver at him and fired twice. Mr Westby staggered back to his bedroom and had time to say just two words – 'Mind yourself' – to his wife Elizabeth, before dropping dead. Mrs Westby opened the bedroom window and cried out for help until neighbours alerted the police. When the police arrived, they found the dead man, his grieving widow and her two daughters, but no sign of the eccentric Henry Jr.

A manhunt was put into place, and a watch kept on any likely location that a fugitive might head for. The next day, the body of William Onions was found in the solicitors' office, and the search for Henry Westby became even more urgent. He had killed twice and might well kill again. Eventually, the strange youth was found hiding in a chicken coop in Lenton Sands. He was persuaded to give himself up, and was taken into custody.

At the inquest and later at the trial, Henry did himself no favours by appearing cold, callous and aloof. When his mother tried to comfort him by putting her hand on his arm, he brushed her off in an irritated and surly manner, telling her not to be soft. He admitted both murders, saying that he had planned for some time to kill his father. 'I am glad he is dead,' he said. 'I could not stand the sight of him. He was always finding fault with me.'

Questioned about the killing of William Onions, he showed even less compassion. Explaining that he had to rehearse the murder of his father to check whether he had the courage to kill, he dismissed the death of the boy with the justification that Onions was continually blowing his nose, spitting and coughing.

Henry Westby's lawyer defended him on the grounds of insanity, though he first had to dissuade Henry from pleading guilty. As evidence of Henry's insanity, the lawyer quoted the fact that his client liked to sleep in a hammock rather than a bed. He bolstered this somewhat thin case by referring to an occasion when Henry had been taken to London but had spent over five hours of the visit sulking in the waiting room of St Pancras Station. Together with the assertion that sane men do not kill their fathers, this was the entire case for the defence; so it is not surprising that the jury found him guilty of murder. Henry showed no emotion, certainly no remorse, as the judge sentenced him to be hanged.

However, his lawyer continued to argue the case for mercy in view of Henry's obvious paranoia, and – unusually for the period – the sentence was eventually commuted, because of the unsound mind of the strange young Nottingham clerk.

3

NURSE
DEATH

The Murders of Louisa and Ada Baguley at Nottingham
May and September 1935

Dorothea Nancy Waddingham was an unprepossessing woman with dark hair drawn into a bun at the nape of her neck, and a gaunt face – described by her contemporaries as horsey. She had heavy-lidded eyes and a yellowish complexion, and she rarely smiled. At one time she had worked in a workhouse infirmary in Burton upon Trent, her duties including cleaning and occasionally serving meals. In 1925, she was charged with the theft of small items, including a number of toothbrushes, and she was put on probation.

She married Tom Leech, a man twice her own age, and the couple set up home with Tom's sister in Church Gresley. Later, they rented a house in Sherwood, Nottingham, furnishing it with items bought on credit. When Dorothea failed to pay any of the money she owed, she once more appeared before magistrates, this time charged with obtaining credit by fraud. Again she was put on probation. When her marriage broke up she resumed her maiden name and took her baby daughter, Mary, to live with a woman friend.

Dorothea Waddingham was inclined to use lies to bolster her position, and she let it be known that she had inherited several thousand pounds from her father. She employed a nursemaid to look after her daughter, but the girl never received any wages. On one occasion, Dorothea offered to get the nursemaid's watch repaired, but she instead pawned it. The girl contacted the police and Dorothea was once again up before a court. This time, she served three months in prison.

The house in Devon Drive where 'Nurse' Waddingham ran her unofficial nursing home. (David Bell)

When she came out, she returned to live with Tom Leech until his death. She then became friendly with one of Tom's friends, Joe Sullivan, an affable, easy-going man. It was at this stage that Dorothea Waddingham – or 'Nurse' Waddingham, as she now styled herself – had a wonderful idea for making money. She suggested to Joe that they use his home in Devon Drive as an establishment for elderly and sick people who needed care. These patients would be easier to look after, she told him, than able-bodied lodgers. She claimed that she herself was an 'unregistered nurse', and said that if any of the patients needed extra medical help, a local doctor could be called in. She would be sure to accept only patients who had enough money to pay the sum of 30 shillings per week for their care.

Joe Sullivan readily agreed to the scheme. Nurse Waddingham moved into 32 Devon Drive, and advertised her home as a caring place for elderly women. A succession of patients moved in but most didn't stay long; they found Nurse Waddingham too severe and overbearing. She had little sympathy for the ill or the elderly, seeing them simply as a source of income. If any of the patients ran out of money, they were evicted immediately.

However, to many elderly women in the outside world, the caring services offered by Nurse Waddingham seemed like a solution to their problems. Mrs Louisa Baguley had spent much of her life caring for her daughter, Ada, who suffered from creeping paralysis. Ada was now middle-aged and wheelchair-bound, and her mother was too old and too infirm to continue to care for her. When Louisa heard about Nurse Waddingham's establishment, she saw it as an answer to her predicament. She went to see Nurse Waddingham, and it was agreed that Ada should move into 32 Devon Drive.

Left on her own, Louisa missed her daughter terribly; she went back to see Dorothea Waddingham and came to a new arrangement: both Baguleys – mother and daughter – would become paying guests in the home. Ada still required medical attention and a local doctor, Dr H. H. Manfield, took over her care. Dorothea's 'nursing' was limited to taking the prescriptions to the chemist and seeing that the patients took their medicine.

It was a great surprise when Nurse Waddingham approached the Baguleys, saying that the cost of their medicines and regular visits from the doctor must be running them short of money. This apparent sympathy from the usually hard-hearted 'Nurse' was a new phenomenon! What Dorothea suggested to Ada Baguley was that she and her mother should pay no more rent for their time at the home. Instead, they would get free care and attention for the rest of their lives in return for a legacy of £1,600 left jointly to Joe Sullivan and Dorothea Waddingham. Although Louisa was nearly 90, Ada was only in her early fifties, so this appeared a financially beneficial arrangement. However long Ada lived, her future care seemed assured.

Nurse Waddingham was in such a good mood that on 6th May 1935 she provided a tin of salmon for Louisa Baguley's tea, to celebrate the Silver Jubilee of George V. On 7th May, the will containing the legacy was drawn up and signed. On 12th May, Ada's mother died. As there were no suspicious circumstances, a death certificate was signed and Mrs Baguley was buried.

As Nurse Waddingham pushed Ada's wheelchair to her mother's funeral, she knew that the £1,600 was a little closer.

It was not long before Dorothea began to bring up the subject of Ada's own funeral arrangements. She told the still-grieving Ada that she thought cremation was a much cleaner and tidier option than burial. Ada agreed, and a letter was written out by Joe Sullivan and signed by Ada. It read: 'I desire to be cremated at my death for health's sake, and it is my wish to remain with Nurse, and my last wish is that my relatives shall not know of my death. Ada Baguley. Witness's name: R. J. Sullivan.'

This letter was addressed to the local doctor, but it was not sent immediately. Nurse Waddingham kept it carefully – along with Ada's will – ready for use when needed.

In early September, Ada had an unexpected visitor, an old friend of her family named Alice Briggs. As the two ladies sat in the garden, talking over old times, and sharing the box of chocolates Alice had brought, Nurse Waddingham watched suspiciously. She wondered what they were talking about. Were they discussing her? Could Ada be thinking of making other arrangements for her future?

After Alice Briggs had gone, Ada was taken ill and during the night, she died. The legacy was now about to fall into Dorothea's hands. All that was left were the formalities.

Dorothea decided that instead of sending Ada's signed letter to the local doctor, she would send it to the Medical Officer of

Health for Nottingham, Dr Cyril Banks. She dispatched it with a covering letter of her own, and made a stupid error. Her letter was headed the Nursing Home, 32 Devon Drive. Just as Dorothea's title of Nurse was an unofficial, self-awarded one, the Nursing Home was a name to which her house was not entitled.

Dr Banks was responsible for the registration of all nursing homes in Nottingham and he knew that 32 Devon Drive was not one of them. When he read the letter signed by Ada Baguley, he noted the request for cremation and the expressed wish to spend her remaining years living at the home of Nurse Waddingham. When he came to Ada's third request – that her relatives should not be informed of her death – he became very suspicious. Nurse Waddingham had again been a little too clever for her own good. Dr Banks contacted the coroner, who ordered an immediate post-mortem.

At the inquest into the death, pathologist Dr Roche Lynch reported that he had conducted the post-mortem and found more than three grammes of morphine in Ada Baguley's body. The inquest jury brought in a verdict that Ada had been murdered, and named Dorothea Waddingham and Joseph Sullivan as the people responsible.

The pair were arrested and brought to trial at Nottingham Assizes before Mr Justice Goddard in February 1936. The prosecution was led by Mr Norman Birkett KC. After considering the evidence, the judge ruled that there was no case against Joseph Sullivan, and Dorothea Waddingham was left to face the charge on her own. She faced a second shock too. She was charged with two murders: that of Louisa Baguley, as well as that of Ada. The authorities had exhumed Louisa's body and found morphine in her remains too.

Dorothea Waddingham had turned up in court looking very maternal with her three-month old baby in her arms, but the child was taken away from her and removed from the court by a nurse – a real nurse, this time. In evidence, Dorothea claimed that the delivery boy who had brought the Baguleys' medicine from the chemist's to her house could have added morphine to it. This extravagant claim was given short shrift by the court. Later, Dorothea went back on her assertion that she had never had any morphine in the house, and stated that Ada Baguley had had ten tablets prescribed for her and had taken only four of them. She thought they were half-grain tablets, as they were just like some she had taken herself when she had pneumonia. She now remembered giving two to Ada Baguley on the evening before she died, as Ada had been suffering from abdominal pains.

Unfortunately for Dorothea Waddingham, she had earlier described how Ada had eaten a heavy meal of roast pork and fruit pie on the evening before she died, and the prosecution invited the jury to speculate on the hearty appetite shown by a woman allegedly suffering from abdominal pain. Again Nurse Waddingham had tried to be too clever. She had told the story of Ada's large evening meal to suggest a possible heart attack brought on by overeating, then contradicted herself by talking of Ada's severe stomach pains when she needed to explain the presence of morphine in the dead woman's body. Dr Manfield gave evidence that he had never prescribed morphine tablets for either of the Baguley ladies.

In view of the evidence, the jury had no difficulty in reaching a verdict of guilty, although they did add a recommendation for mercy. Mr Justice Goddard ignored the recommendation, and sentenced Dorothea Waddingham to death. The defence appealed against the verdict, claiming that the judge had omitted to mention to the jury the possibility of bringing in a manslaughter verdict. The Lord Chief Justice rejected the appeal on the grounds that a manslaughter verdict would have been impossible in this case, and the judge was therefore quite right not to mention it.

'Nurse' Waddingham was hanged in Winson Green Prison, Birmingham, on 16th April 1936.

4

MISSING
CHILD

The Murder of Mona Tinsley at Hayton, near Retford
January 1937

After the Christmas holidays, ten year old Mona Tinsley went back to school on Monday 4th January 1937. She was in Miss Hawley's class at the Wesleyan Methodist School in Guildhall Street, Newark-on-Trent. On her first day back, she resumed her normal routine: she arrived at school for 9 am, went home for dinner, returned to school, and walked home again at 4 pm. It took her about 20 minutes to walk to her home in Thoresby Street, so she was home by 4.30 pm. However, when she came out of the school the next day, she saw a figure waiting at the gate. He seemed to be waiting for her, but Mona was not alarmed because it was her 'Uncle Fred' – not a real uncle, but a man who used to lodge at her house. She was surprised to see him in Newark, as Uncle Fred had moved away over a year ago. She went over to him and began to chat.

When Mona failed to return home that afternoon, her mother was not too worried at first. The Tinsleys had several relations living in the area, and it was not unknown for Mona to call on one of them on her way home from school. Once when she had called at a house where there were seven new kittens, she had forgotten the time and had not arrived home until after 6 o'clock.

By 7 o'clock, however, Mona was still not home and her parents began to walk round to the homes of all the relatives where Mona might be, but no one had seen her. It was 9 o'clock before Mona's father gave in to his fears and contacted the police. Harry Barnes, the Chief Constable of the Newark force, put an immediate search for the missing child into operation.

25

Officers scoured the banks of the river Trent, and looked into sheds, garages and empty properties throughout the town.

The next day, all the local schools were informed of Mona's disappearance, and the staff and children were asked if they had seen the girl on the Tuesday afternoon. One boy, William Plackett, who coincidentally lived next door to the Tinsleys, volunteered the information that he had seen Mona with a man near the bus station. His description of the man was rather vague, but later that day, Mrs Annie Hird, another neighbour from Thoresby Street, contacted the police to say that she had seen a man waiting outside Mona's school shortly before 4 o'clock on the Tuesday afternoon. Mrs Hird's evidence was more helpful: she had recognised the man as the Tinsleys' former lodger, Frederick Nodder.

The police began to investigate Nodder's background. He had left his wife some years previously, and there was a court order against him for non-payment of maintenance for an illegitimate child. In 1935, Nodder had gone to lodge with a Mr and Mrs Grimes in Sheffield. A year later he came to Newark-on-Trent to lodge with Mrs Tinsley, who was Mrs Grimes's sister. He was a car mechanic, but he had long periods without work, because of his intemperance and dishonesty. After a few weeks in the Tinsley household, no rent money had been forthcoming and Mrs Tinsley had asked Fred to leave. He had then moved to a village near Retford, in the north of the county.

Inquiries at Newark bus depot brought the police more evidence. Charles Neville had been driving the bus from Newark to Retford on the afternoon in question, and remembered picking up a young girl dressed in a brown coat, who was in the company of a middle-aged man. The man had bought a single fare for the girl, but a return ticket for himself. They had got off the bus together at Grove Street, in the middle of Retford.

Police attempts to track down Nodder's address were initially hampered by Mrs Grimes's reluctance to give them any help, which seemed extraordinary in view of the fact that they were investigating the disappearance of her own niece. Later, however, she admitted that she and Nodder had once had an affair. Gossip soon spread that Mona might in fact be their natural daughter, but the police were quickly able to discount that theory, and to scotch the untrue rumour.

Frederick Nodder's house in Hayton. (David Bell)

Inquiries in Retford established that Fred Nodder now lived by himself in a rented semi-detached house in Smeath Lane in the village of Hayton. Ironically, the house was called Peacehaven. Police went to Smeath Lane, where they spoke to one of Nodder's neighbours, Doreen Jarman, who said that she had seen a girl outside the back door of Peacehaven at midday on Wednesday 6th January, while Fred Nodder had been working in his garden. The girl was wearing a skirt and a blue jumper, and Doreen thought she looked about eight or nine.

Chief Constable Harry Barnes went to Peacehaven, together with other officers, and waited for Fred Nodder to return home. He eventually turned up at 11 pm, and he was immediately questioned about Mona Tinsley's disappearance. Nodder admitted that he knew the girl, but said that he had not seen her since he left his lodgings in Newark, 15 months earlier. The police were not satisfied with his statement; Nodder was arrested on a holding charge – his unpaid affiliation warrant – and taken to Newark police station for further questioning. At an identity parade the next day, he was picked out by several passengers who had travelled on the bus from Newark to Retford, as well as by William Plackett and Annie Hird.

Faced with this evidence, Fred Nodder decided to change his story. He admitted talking to Mona outside her school in Newark on the Tuesday afternoon, but claimed that she had asked him to take her to Sheffield to visit her aunt, Mrs Grimes, and her baby cousin. He had agreed with her request and taken her to Retford, but had then become reluctant to go as far as Sheffield, where there was a court order against him. He claimed that he had taken Mona on another bus as far as Worksop, and there left her to catch a bus to Sheffield by herself. If anyone had harmed the girl, it was not him. It must have been someone she met on the bus from Worksop to Sheffield.

This new story seemed ludicrous. He was now claiming that he had sent a ten year old girl alone on a 19 mile bus journey, to be followed by a tram ride across Sheffield, on a dark January night, on her way to visit an aunt who was not expecting her. The improbability of the tale made it look as though he was actually saying to the police, 'You know I did it – Now try and prove it.'

When the police found some paper with Mona's handwriting and drawings on it in the house in Hayton, together with a child's handkerchief and unwashed crockery bearing a child's finger-prints, they were even more convinced that Fred Nodder had killed Mona. However, they needed a body to prove it.

Recalling the neighbours' comments about Nodder gardening while a child was there, they began digging up the entire garden. Finding nothing, they now knew that they faced a mammoth task. They dragged the Chesterfield canal, which ran near Nodder's home, and the nearby river Idle. They searched pits and quarries, and opened trunks and boxes left at the railway station. With the help of 900 volunteers from the Retford area, they searched hedgerows and woods. The whole countryside around Hayton was combed, including parts of Sherwood Forest. All the efforts proved fruitless, however, and when Frederick Nodder was taken to court on 10th January he was charged with abduction, taking a child 'by force or fraud', but not with murder.

He was remanded to appear at Birmingham Assizes in March,

and the trial took place before Mr Justice Swift. Nodder's defence was that he had not taken Mona away by force or fraud because the girl had asked him to take her to her aunt's house and therefore had gone of her own free will. His claim that he had accompanied her to Worksop, then sent her on to Sheffield, was undermined by the evidence of several passengers who had travelled on the Worksop–Sheffield bus on the night in question. None of them had seen a child – alone or accompanied – on that bus. After a two-day trial, the jury took less than 20 minutes to bring in a guilty verdict. Sentencing Nodder, the judge stated, 'You have been found guilty of a dreadful crime. What you did with that little girl, what became of her, only you know. It may be that time will reveal the dreadful secret which you carry in your breast. I cannot tell, but I am determined that so far as I have part in that dreadful tragedy of the 5th and 6th January, I will keep you in custody.' So saying, he sentenced Nodder to seven years in prison.

The words of Mr Justice Swift were to prove prophetic. Exactly five months after Mona Tinsley's disappearance, her body was discovered in the river Idle. It was a sunny Sunday afternoon, and Walter Marshall was rowing his family on a leisurely trip along the river when he noticed an object in the water. He manoeuvred nearer and was shocked to find that it was a child's body, trapped in mud and weeds. He rowed to the bank and sent his son for the police. PC Sheridan arrived and, with Walter Marshall's help, he managed to get the body out of the water and onto the bank. It was the body of a young girl, and had obviously been in the river for some months. Superintendent Burkitt arrived to take charge, and the body was taken to the Ship Inn at Newington where it was later identified by Mona Tinsley's father. Apart from the coat and one missing wellington boot, Mona was dressed in the same clothes she had been wearing when she disappeared.

The post-mortem carried out by pathologist Dr James Webster established that Mona had been strangled by a ligature before being put into the water. The decomposition of the body made it impossible to tell whether she had been sexually assaulted. Mona Tinsley was buried at the Methodist church in Newark on 20th July 1937.

Frederick Nodder was charged with her murder, and was tried at Nottingham Assizes on 22nd November. The prosecution alleged that on the afternoon of Tuesday 5th January Nodder had taken the child from Newark to Retford and then on to his home in Hayton. He had kept her there overnight, and had probably abused her. The next day he had strangled her, perhaps after realising that his neighbour had spotted the girl. He had then wrapped the body in sacking and carried it across fields, across a canal bridge, until he reached the river Idle. There he had put the body into the river, ramming it into an underwater drain so that it could not float to the top. When the police had dragged the river in January, it had been a swollen torrent and they had failed to find Mona's body, but by June the river was much lower, thus allowing the boating party to make their grim discovery. After disposing of his victim, Nodder had gone for a drink and then returned to his house to find the police waiting for him.

Like the first trial, this one lasted two days. Once more the jury found Nodder guilty, and this time the judge donned the black cap to sentence the accused to death. 'Justice', said Mr Justice Macnaghten, 'has slowly overtaken you.' Nodder was hanged in Lincoln Prison on 30th December 1937.

One of the features of the case that appealed greatly to the newspapers of the time was the part played by spiritualist medium Estelle Roberts. Estelle approached the police in January, soon after Mona Tinsley's disappearance, telling them that she had been visited by the spirit of the dead girl. At first the authorities were reluctant to accept her offers of help, although they did 'unofficially' let her have one of Mona's frocks to hold while supposedly contacting the girl. Later, Estelle Roberts was allowed to speak to Mona's parents in Newark, and she was also taken by the police to Nodder's house in Hayton.

There – aided by Red Cloud, her native American spirit guide – she described to them how the girl had been assaulted and murdered. The police were surprised, and reluctantly impressed, when Estelle Roberts was able to tell them things about the house that she could not have known, and they were therefore willing to accompany her when she tried to follow the route along which the body had been carried from the house. She led the police officers across the canal bridge and into muddy fields before losing the trail. However, she did say that there was a river somewhere ahead, where the body was lying. The police searched the river, but because of flooding, they had been unable to find any trace of the girl's body at that time.

5

THE
WOULD-BE POET

The Murder of Mabel Tattershaw at
Sherwood Vale, Nottingham
August 1951

At about 4 pm on 4th August 1951, the *News of the World* newspaper in Fleet Street received a call from a public phone-box in Nottingham. The caller – a man – said that he wanted to speak to someone about a murder, and the switchboard operator put the call through to Norman Rae, the paper's chief crime reporter. When Norman asked the caller which murder he wanted to talk about, he was surprised to be told that it was a 'new' case, one the police didn't yet know about.

The caller introduced himself as Herbert Mills. He said that he had found the body of a strangled woman, and wanted to know how much the newspaper would pay for an exclusive account. Mills said that he was thinking of a figure around £250.

Norman Rae knew that he had to tell the police, but he didn't wish to lose contact with his informant. If Herbert Mills really had found the body of a murder victim, there certainly could be an exclusive story for the newspaper. He had to stall. He told Herbert Mills that he couldn't agree terms until he'd spoken to his editor, and asked him to phone back in 30 minutes. To the reporter's relief, Mills agreed before hanging up.

Norman Rae rang the Nottingham City police headquarters immediately, and described his strange phone call. He was asked to keep the caller talking when he rang back, so that the Nottingham detectives could trace the call and pick up the

31

informant. Herbert Mills must have been impatient to sell his story, because it was far less than half an hour before he telephoned again. At first, Norman refused to give Mills a definite answer to his proposal, and kept him busy with a number of questions.

Herbert Mills told the reporter that he often went to Sherwood Vale to write poetry. On this occasion he had found a bead necklace on the ground and as he stooped to pick it up he had spotted, out of the corner of his eye, the body of a woman. The face was very white and pale, he recalled, and the woman seemed dead. He had been startled by his discovery and wondered what to do next. He had left the spot and headed home, pausing on the way to sit on a bank and read Shelley's 'Ode to Death'. Then he had thought of phoning the *News of the World* to offer his story.

Norman refrained from telling the caller how pretentious he sounded, and instead spoke enthusiastically about using Herbert's information. He mentioned letting the would-be author write the article himself, and suggested themes he might include. While the two men were still talking on the phone, the Nottingham police arrived at the call-box and took Herbert Mills into custody.

At police headquarters, Herbert told detectives that his full name was Herbert Leonard Mills and he was 19 years old. He seemed frank and open as he claimed that everything he had told Norman Rae was true. He reaffirmed that he often went to Sherwood Vale to read and write poetry and that, on the morning of 8th August, he had found a woman's body there. When the police officers seemed somewhat sceptical about his story, Herbert reached into his pocket and produced a string of beads, claiming he had found them near the body.

The police drove Mills back to Sherwood Vale, where they accompanied him as he walked purposefully along a narrow track to a deep gully full of weeds. He pointed down into the gully at a coat. When the police pulled the coat back, Mills's story proved correct. Beneath the coat was the body of a middle-aged woman. She had a bruise on her blackened and bloated face, and marks on her throat and neck. Her protruding eyes and tongue indicated that she might have been strangled.

In a pocket of the coat, the police found a receipt with the name Mrs Tattershaw and an address in Longmead Drive, Nottingham. The police went to that address and discovered that Mrs Mabel Tattershaw – a 48 year old mother of two – had not been seen by her neighbours for over a week. She had disappeared on Friday 3rd August after going to the cinema. Further inquiries established that she had been seen on the Thursday afternoon in the Roxy cinema in conversation with a man sitting next to her, though the descriptions of this mystery man were rather vague.

Herbert Mills was again questioned by detectives and then, after a stern warning about his foolish behaviour in failing to inform the police about his discovery of the body, he was released.

He immediately renewed his contacts with the *News of the World*, and Norman Rae came up to Nottingham to interview him. They met in a café, then later went for a drink in the old Black Boy public house. Herbert was very scornful of the efforts of the police, sneering at a press statement that they were looking for 'a man with a limp'. Norman managed not to stare at Mills's twisted right foot.

Herbert travelled back to London with Norman Rae and stayed with another reporter from the same newspaper. The *News of the World* did not want him talking to other papers. He was taken to the Festival of Britain and shown round the West End. He went to the theatre to see *King's Rhapsody* and was given £5 spending money.

Later, when he returned to Nottingham, he was given a further £75. This was not as much as he had expected, and he tried to sell various bits of extra information to the paper. He told them that press reports of Mrs Tattershaw being battered to death were wrong; she had been strangled. Herbert Mills was quite correct: Mrs Tattershaw had been strangled, but at this stage the police themselves were not completely sure of the cause of death. Mills seemed to know more than they did.

At the inquest into Mrs Tattershaw's death, Herbert Mills gave his evidence confidently and coolly. When the coroner commented that it seemed incredible that a person finding a body should try to make money from it rather than call the police, Mills seemed imperturbed by the criticism.

The police had their suspicions about some of Herbert Mills's

Herbert Mills arriving at the inquest. (Nottinghamshire Local Studies Library)

statements. He had said that the white face of the dead woman had first attracted his attention, whereas the face had been bruised and blackened when the police found it. However, there was still no real evidence to connect Herbert Mills to the killing.

In the end, the verbose young man talked himself into the dock. In his numerous conversations with Norman Rae, he boasted of many things: having a perfect system to beat the bookies was one of his claims. When the reporter seemed to be losing interest – after all, the story of the body was now yesterday's news – Mills played his trump card. Sitting in the Black Boy on 25th August, he confessed to the murder. He told how he had sat next to the lonely woman in the Roxy cinema. When he had started talking to her, she had seemed flattered at his attentions and agreed to meet him the next day outside another cinema, the Metropole. On the Friday afternoon, the couple had gone for a walk, and had ended up at Sherwood Vale, in an area of overgrown orchard known locally as 'the jungle'.

There, Mills decided to put into effect one of his fantasies: he would commit the perfect murder. He talked her into lying down – a request which the woman no doubt interpreted as a prelude to making love. Mills placed two coats over her, so that she would not get any threads from his clothing under her fingernails. He put on a pair of gloves, knelt on her shoulders and proceeded to punch her in the face before strangling her. Mills could not resist adding in his confession: 'I was rather pleased. I thought I did it rather well.' After murdering Mrs Tattershaw, the young man slid the body down into a gully and covered it with one of the coats before going home. He waited five more days, contemplating his perfect crime, before telephoning the *News of the World* and offering to sell them the story of how he had 'found' the body.

Sitting in the Black Boy, listening to the young man's confession, Norman Rae produced paper and asked him to write it all down. This he did. Norman then accompanied him to the police station, where he gave the confession to Superintendent Percy Ellington.

Herbert Mills was charged with murder and appeared before Mr Justice Byrne at Nottingham Assizes the following November. His confession shocked the jury, particularly the part that read: 'I had always considered the possibility of committing the perfect crime, murder. I am very much interested in crime. Here was my opportunity. I have been most successful, no motive, no clues. Why, if I had not reported finding the body I should not have been connected in any manner whatsoever. I am quite proud of my achievement.' However, the confession was not the only evidence. Two witnesses had seen Mabel Tattershaw and Herbert Mills walking together along Mansfield Road towards Sherwood Vale on the evening of the murder. Also, fibres from Mills's clothing were found on Mrs Tattershaw's body. His device of covering her with coats before killing her had not been as clever as he had anticipated. Nevertheless, he might have got away with it, if it had not been for that part of his personality which demanded that, after committing the crime, he had to draw attention to it. It was not enough for Herbert Mills that he thought he had committed the perfect crime: he had to tell people how clever he had been.

When the jury brought in a unanimous verdict of guilty, the judge donned the black cap and sentenced him to death. Mills, still cocky, still composed, smiled at the judge and jury and winked at his own father. In Lincoln Prison, he laughed as he watched his grave being dug. On the day of his execution, he laughed as he asked the hangman to make a good job of it. In this he was disappointed: it took him 20 slow minutes to die, a sight which caused the doctor present to become a campaigner for the abolition of capital punishment.

6

'THE STORY AS OLD AS TIME'

The Murder of Maureen Lee at Southwell
April 1970

As Stan Cartman was driving out of Duke's Wood, between Eakring and Kirklington, on the afternoon of 8th April 1970, he saw a woman lying on the ground. She was only about ten yards from the road, and her handbag was standing upright on the grass nearby. He stopped and got out of his van, thinking at first that she was sleeping. He called out to her but got no reply. When he realised that she was dead, he drove back to the BP oil depot where he worked as a pipefitter, and rang the police.

It did not take the police long to identify the body as that of 28 year old Mrs Maureen Lee, who had been reported missing from her home in Southwell nine days earlier. Her husband, Anthony Lee, a lecturer at Brackenhurst Agricultural College, told the police that he had not seen his wife since she walked out of their bungalow on the evening of Easter Monday, saying that she was fed up. He added that this was following 'a small row' over who should take the children to school. He had reported her missing when she had not returned home the next day, 31st March. The police had already established that auburn-haired Maureen Lee had not visited friends or relatives after her disappearance, and she had not left Southwell by bus.

A post-mortem, conducted by Home Office pathologist Dr Alan Usher, established that the cause of Maureen Lee's death was strangulation by a ligature around her neck. She had not been sexually assaulted.

On 8th April, the day the body was discovered, Anthony Lee

The spot in Duke's Wood, near Eakring, where the body of Maureen Lee was found. (*Newark Advertiser*)

Anthony Lee was a lecturer at Brackenhurst Agricultural College. His lover was a student there. (David Bell)

was interviewed at Southwell police station by Detective Chief Superintendent Thomas McCullough, head of Nottinghamshire CID, and Detective Superintendent James Whitehead. At 10 o'clock that evening, he was charged with the murder of his wife. He made a three-minute court appearance before magistrates at Newark the following day, and was remanded in custody.

Anthony Lee's trial took place at Nottingham Assizes three months later, before Mr Justice Cusack. The prosecution counsel, Mr P. J. Cox QC, told the court that Anthony and Maureen Lee were married in 1961, having known each other since childhood. He became a lecturer at Brackenhurst Agricultural College in Southwell in July 1968, and a year later he began an association with a 21 year old female student there, telling her that his marriage had deteriorated since the birth of his fourth child. The friendship with this student developed into a passionate affair, and in October 1969 he told her that he was going to ask his wife for a divorce. He twice moved out of the family home and into lodgings, so that he could continue the affair with the student. In February he told his girlfriend that he had agreed to return home to his family, but he would be sleeping apart from his wife.

It was at this stage that the Lee family moved into their bungalow in Southwell. Anthony Lee told his lover that he was very depressed and was still having rows with his wife, but was unable to persuade her to consent to a divorce. On 1st April he sent a letter to the girl saying that his wife had walked out. A few days later, he told his girlfriend that he had informed the police that their love affair had ended in February; he suggested that, if interviewed, she should stick to the same story.

Maureen Lee had not been seen since Easter Monday, the court was informed. On that day, a neighbour saw Maureen, Anthony and the four children out for 'a normal, happy family walk' with their two dogs. Early the next day, Anthony phoned an old friend and told him that Maureen had walked out the previous evening after a row about who should take the children to school. Later that day, he informed the police that his wife was missing, and a missing person report was circulated. He suggested to the police that they should make a search, in case Maureen had tried to hitch a lift and had ended up lying in a wood or in a river.

Several days later, Mrs Lee's body was indeed found lying in a wood at Duke's Wood, about five miles from her home.

Although Lee had, when first interviewed, adhered to the story of his wife walking out after a row, he eventually told Detective Chief Superintendent Thomas McCullough that after the quarrel, Maureen had called his girlfriend a cow, and kept 'on and on'. He told Tom McCullough that Maureen was a mother before everything else, and she pampered the children too much. There was no one he could turn to. 'I don't know what possessed me to do it,' he said.

Asked by the detective, 'To do what?' Anthony Lee replied, 'To kill her.' He explained that he had picked up an apron from beside the bed and held it round her. When she went limp, he had sat on the side of the bed and 'cried his eyes out'. He described dressing her and putting the body into the boot of the car, then driving to Eakring. He told Tom McCullough that he was very sorry, and that his life had been a nightmare ever since.

Mr Harry Skinner QC, the defence counsel, told the court that he would not be seeking an acquittal, but would be asking for a verdict of manslaughter. Called to give evidence in his own defence, Anthony Lee said that when he and his wife married, he

Anthony Lee. (*Newark Advertiser*)

was managing a small farm on behalf of his father-in-law. Since then, he had qualified as a teacher and obtained a post as a lecturer at an agricultural college. After their fourth child was born, in May 1968, his wife had lost all interest in the sexual side of the marriage. He had met a young lady in September 1969, when she was taking a field course at his college, and they had become lovers. In November, he left his wife and went to live with his girlfriend in a farm cottage at Caunton, but his wife begged him to come back to her and, in February, he did.

Lee said that, after a row on the evening of Easter Monday, he and his wife went to bed at 11.30 pm. Maureen had started to raise matters from the past, going from one subject to another. He felt depressed and asked her to stop. She turned over and lay with her back to him, and he was thinking of the things she had been saying. He saw an apron at the side of the bed and picked it up. Intending to frighten her, he put it around her neck. While agreeing that he wanted a divorce, he denied that it had ever crossed his mind that one way out of his situation was to do away with his wife. He partially dressed his wife's body and took her to the place where it was found.

Asked why he had lied to the police, telling them – and others – that his wife had walked out on him, Lee said that he was frightened of the consequences. He also said that he had never shown any violence towards his wife, 'not even slapping her'. Cross-examined by the prosecution, Lee admitted that he had told the police that his affair had ended in February, but claimed that this was in order to protect his girlfriend, not to remove a possible motive for murder. He agreed that he had wanted a divorce in order to marry the girl.

Summing up, the judge told the jury that it was essential in cases of this kind that they should face realities and exercise a knowledge of human nature. He said that they should consider whether the story they had heard was not in fact 'the story as old as time – a husband who commits adultery, a wife who dares to protest, is desperately unhappy, who gets in the way, and is eventually disposed of'. He said they should also consider whether Mrs Lee was actually asleep when her husband put the apron around her neck. He reminded them that Lee had left his wife's handbag by her body in the wood, and asked whether this was an attempt to make it appear that his wife had been attacked and killed in circumstances that had nothing to do with him. The judge pointed out that Lee had left his wife's body in a place where it would be found before long, and suggested that, as Lee was eager to marry his girlfriend, this might have been easier with a dead wife, rather than a missing one.

The jury retired for a little under two hours, before bringing in a verdict that Anthony Lee was guilty of murder. Addressing Lee, Mr Justice Cusack told him, 'You have been found guilty of murder on very clear evidence. The law permits only one sentence in such circumstances. The sentence is that you be imprisoned for life.'

7

IN
THE LINE OF DUTY

The Murder of PC Christopher McDonald at Worksop

May 1978

Peter Loveday and Tony 'Jock' Cherrie were an ill-matched pair of villains. In May 1978, Peter, a 19 year old absconder from Borstal, had met up with Jock Cherrie in a London pub. Jock was 36, and had a long criminal record. His violent past was written on his face, in his scarred lips and broken nose. Despite the differences in their ages and criminal experience, the two men decided to team up to commit robberies. Since Peter did not want the authorities calling at his home in New Cross, the two men stole a car and headed north for Derbyshire. Peter Loveday had been born in Chesterfield, and he had a married cousin, Peter Culley, living in Creswell. They could stay with him, and with a bit of luck, persuade him to join them in their activities.

On the morning of Monday 16th May, the three men set out from Creswell for Worksop, five miles away, to look for likely premises to rob. In Central Avenue, they came across a jewellery shop, Gryska's, attached to Vanessa Hair Salon. It looked promising. The windows and doors of Gryska's looked secure, but if they broke into the hairdresser's, they might be able to get through the adjoining wall to the more lucrative jeweller's. At 8.30 that night they returned, parking their getaway car in King Street. They managed to get into Vanessa's, where Jock Cherrie helped himself to £18 from the till. The wall between the two shops proved too substantial for their efforts, however, so they decided to go via the roof. Cherrie and Culley went down into the building to try to break into the jewellery shop, leaving Peter

The river Ryton where PC Chris McDonald's body was found. (David Bell)

Loveday on the roof to keep watch. It was not long before Peter heard a burglar alarm begin to sound, and soon after that he saw a police officer approaching through the fog.

PC Christopher McDonald was on night duty, patrolling a beat in the centre of Worksop. At about 12.15 am, the police received a report from a neighbouring householder that a burglar alarm was sounding on the premises of Gryska's the jeweller's. Responding to the alarm call, 19 year old Chris McDonald hurried to the scene, and soon radioed to control that he was in contact with the offenders. At 12.28 am he reported that he was pursuing one of the offenders across the river towards the cricket ground. The river Ryton, 12 feet wide but only three feet deep, ran behind the shops, with Worksop cricket ground across the other side of the water.

That was the last communication received from the young officer, and when he failed to respond to calls, a team of police officers, some with tracker dogs, mounted a search; they found the missing man's helmet in a yard near the jeweller's. Eight hours after his final message, the officer's body was discovered in the mist-shrouded river, with a large, $8\frac{3}{4}$ lb old-style house-brick lying on his face, at a spot 200 yards from the jeweller's shop. His truncheon was missing, though he was still in possession of his handcuffs and radio. His pocket notebook was floating on the water nearby.

PC McDonald's body was taken to Worksop Victoria Hospital, where Home Office pathologist Dr Alan Usher carried out a post-mortem. He found 21 marks of injury on the officer's body, most of them wounds to the neck, face and head. He had been left unconscious in the water and death was actually caused by drowning.

Charles MacLachlan, the Chief Constable of Nottinghamshire, issued a statement in which he said that Christopher McDonald had been an extremely promising young officer who would be sadly missed. He continued, 'The whole force is in a state of shock following the incident, which is yet another example of the devotion to duty and complete disregard to personal safety displayed by members of this force.' It was revealed that Christopher McDonald had joined the police as a cadet two years earlier and had become a probationer constable in September 1977. He had been stationed at Worksop for only three months.

One of Christopher's closest friends, PC Wayne Anderson, said that the dead policeman was always prepared to have a go and could handle himself well. 'He was kind and gentle, a really nice lad,' he added.

The police search for the killer of PC McDonald was greatly helped when, on the day the body was found, a bus conductress became suspicious of one of her passengers. The bus was travelling from Creswell to Chesterfield, and at 1.50 pm it picked up a young man who came running from the direction of Worksop Road. Miss Maureen Saxton intuitively felt there was something odd about the man, who seemed very much 'on edge'. She informed the driver, Stanley Disney, about her feelings and when the bus stopped at Clowne, he phoned a message to the police.

When the bus reached Chesterfield, it was met by two detective constables, and Mr Disney pointed out to them the passenger whose behaviour had been so strange. The man told the officers that his name was Peter Loveday and admitted that he was an absconder from Borstal. During this discussion, Loveday suddenly ran off. He was caught in a cul-de-sac, and

Christopher McDonald. (*Nottingham Post*)

after a violent struggle the 18-stone Loveday was arrested and taken to the police station.

Interviewed by Chief Superintendent Roy Readwin, head of Nottinghamshire CID, Loveday admitted that he had been on the roof of the jeweller's in Worksop with two other men, 'when a bobby came along'. After a fight, in which he had hit the policeman with his fist, he and his two companions had run away across the river. The police officer had pursued them, catching up with them in the river and hitting Loveday on the shoulder with his truncheon. A second fight ensued, in which one of Loveday's companions took the truncheon away from the officer and knocked him down with it. Loveday claimed that all three men had been hitting the policeman. They had left the officer thrashing about in the water, close to the bank of the river, before running away and splitting up. It was obvious to the detectives that this account did not tally with the discovery of Christopher McDonald's body under the water of the river Ryton with a brick on his face.

In a later interview, when asked what had really happened, a sobbing Loveday confessed that he was the only one involved in the fight with PC McDonald. The true version of events was that Loveday's two companions had already got away when PC McDonald had caught up with him in the river. When the officer struck him with the truncheon, Loveday had fallen into the water and had found a house-brick. He had used this to smash the officer on the head twice, before hitting him a number of times with the truncheon. He could not remember how many times he had struck the officer. He had left him unconscious in the river, but did not know whether he was dead at the time.

Gradually, the police pieced together Loveday's movements after leaving the river. At a builder's premises in King Street, the owner found a pool of water on the floor, together with damp pieces of curtain. Peter Loveday had dried himself here, after his fight in the river. A bus driver on the early-morning run from Worksop to Bakeston Moor reported picking up a man who had paid his fare with coins covered with wet mud. Mrs Annie Culley, the wife of Loveday's cousin, gave the police valuable information about what happened when Loveday returned to her home, some hours after the return of her husband and Jock Cherrie.

Peter Culley was immediately arrested by the police; it was some weeks before they could trace Tony Cherrie who had returned to London, but eventually he too was arrested.

The funeral of PC Christopher McDonald was held on Friday 23rd June at Worksop Priory. Accompanied by a slow drum beat, the funeral procession through the streets of Worksop was preceded by six mounted police officers, with other colleagues walking alongside the coffin, which was draped with a Union Jack and bore Christopher's police helmet. Among the 1,200 people who attended were 500 police officers from 30 different forces. There were family mourners, including Christopher's parents, his two younger sisters, and his girlfriend. The service was conducted by Canon Peter Boulton, the lesson was read by the Chief Constable, and an address was given by the Bishop of Southwell. Among the mourners were the Lord Lieutenant of the county, and local MPs Joe Ashton and William Whitlock. After the official service there was a private service at St Andrew's church in Skegby, Christopher's home town, followed by cremation in Mansfield.

In October, Loveday appeared at Nottingham Crown Court before Mr Justice Pain, and pleaded not guilty to a charge of murder. He also denied two joint charges of burglary, and his case was adjourned for trial. At the same court, his cousin Peter John Culley and his friend Anthony McCracken Cherrie pleaded guilty to a charge of stealing £18 from Vanessa Hair Salon, and attempting to break into Gryska jeweller's in Central Avenue, Worksop. The prosecution said that the Crown took the view that neither man had any part in the murder of PC McDonald. Chief Superintendent Roy Readwin told the court that both men had been co-operative with the police and had made helpful statements. The judge said that Culley had been drawn into the enterprise by Cherrie, who had an appalling record. Peter Culley was sentenced to 18 months in prison, and Jock Cherrie received three years.

In February 1979, Peter Loveday appeared once more at Nottingham Crown Court, this time before Mr Justice Drake, charged with the murder of PC Christopher McDonald. He was also charged with burglary; he now pleaded guilty on the burglary charge but continued to plead not guilty to murder. The prosecuting counsel, Mr Percy Grieve QC, called Mrs Annie

Culley as a witness. She told the court that on the morning of Tuesday 17th May 1978, she had come downstairs to find her husband's cousin, Peter Loveday, sitting on the settee dressed only in a towel. He told her that he had hit a policeman on the head with a brick and with a truncheon. The policeman had ended up under the water with his mouth open, and Loveday said he had held him down in the water until he drowned. Annie Culley stated that she did not believe him at first because she knew that he tended to 'tell a lot of stories', but she then heard about the death of the policeman on the television news. When her husband and Jock Cherrie heard the news, they swore at Peter Loveday and called him names for being stupid. Loveday then left the house.

Cross-examined by Mr Denis Cowley QC, Mrs Culley denied making up the story because Loveday had implicated her husband.

Peter Loveday gave evidence that he had been petrified when he heard on the television news that the policeman who had chased him had been murdered. He denied telling Mrs Culley that he had 'done him in'; he had simply told her that he had been in a fight with 'the Old Bill', hitting the constable with a brick and then running away. He said that he had no intention of killing or injuring the policeman; he only wanted to get away. He said that in his initial statement he had falsely implicated his accomplices because he was scared. He claimed that he had never told the police that the officer was unconscious when he left him. He complained that he had been ill treated by the police, who kept digging him in the chest and had made him take a cold bath without soap or a towel.

The detectives who had arrested Loveday when he got off the bus in Chesterfield denied that he had been ill treated in any way. Chief Superintendent Readwin told the jury that, when charged with the murder, Loveday had replied, 'I am sorry. It just happened on the spur of the moment.' Readwin agreed with the defence counsel that Loveday had no previous record of violence.

After a four-day trial, Mr Justice Drake told the jury that they would have to consider whether Loveday had intended to kill or seriously injure PC McDonald. If they thought he had not, or if they were not sure, then they should return a verdict of manslaughter. However, if they believed that he meant the blows to kill or cause serious injury, or if they thought that he had held the officer under the water, then they must bring in a verdict of murder.

The jury retired for 95 minutes before bringing in a unanimous verdict of murder. The judge told Loveday that he had been found guilty of murder on the clearest possible evidence, and sentenced him to life imprisonment. He also sentenced him to a concurrent sentence of three years on each of the two admitted charges of burglary.

In 1979, the Christopher McDonald memorial trust fund was established. This fund provides training and educational scholarships for regular officers or cadet members of Nottinghamshire Constabulary to study policing methods, at home or abroad. Christopher's father, who was appointed a trustee, said at the launch on 1st February, 'For as long as I can remember, Christopher lived for the day when he joined the police service and talked of nothing but his career. The Trust will not only be a fitting memorial to Christopher, but will also, I hope, give other youngsters added encouragement and a sense of great pride in the police service.'

In 1980, PC McDonald was posthumously awarded the Queen's Commendation for Bravery.

8

THE
SURVIVALIST

The Murder of George Luckett at Girton
June 1982

When the killer came south from Yorkshire into Nottinghamshire in June 1982, he had already shot dead one policeman and held captive an elderly woman. He was obsessed with the SAS, and with methods of evading capture and living off the land. His favourite reading matter was *No Need to Die*, a book on survivalist techniques written by ex-paratrooper Eddie McGee.

On Thursday 17th June, PC David Haigh had been shot dead while checking a green Citroën car at Norwood Edge, a picnic spot near Harrogate in North Yorkshire. The police quickly linked the vehicle involved with a car of the same colour and make seen six days earlier in Lindsey Forest, Lincolnshire, when a gamekeeper had asked its driver to move on. The gamekeeper had noted the registration number of the car, KYF 326P. PC Haigh had written down the same registration number – together with a false name for the driver – on the morning that he was shot. It was later to transpire that the man who had given PC Haigh a false name before shooting him dead, had, strangely enough, given his correct date of birth.

Three days after the murder of the police constable, the Citroën was found abandoned, hidden in the middle of a wheat field at Ledsham, near Garforth, West Yorkshire. There was no sign of the driver. The same day, 75 year old Mrs Veda Jackson was attacked and tied up at her home in Blyton Carr, on the outskirts of Lindsey Forest.

On Tuesday 22nd June, the killer – who was now in rural east

Police officers search the field opposite George Luckett's bungalow in Girton. (*Newark Advertiser*)

Nottinghamshire – desperately needed another car. He entered the isolated bungalow home of George and Sylvia Luckett in Girton, about eight miles north of Newark. Mr and Mrs Luckett had lived in the quiet, rural village on the east bank of the river Trent for some years.

The intruder tied up the middle-aged couple, then went outside to check how much petrol was in their car. When he returned, the killer shot George first, and then Sylvia, before driving away in their car, a brown 2.6 litre Rover with the registration number VAU 875S.

Although George was dead, his wife was not. Despite being severely injured, with a bullet lodged near her brain, Sylvia Luckett managed to free herself six hours after the attack. With incredible courage she staggered half a mile to a neighbour's house to raise the alarm.

Sylvia was rushed to Derby Royal Infirmary for surgery to

remove the bullet, while the Nottinghamshire police began a murder hunt to find her husband's killer. When scientists at the forensic laboratories in Nottingham established that the bullets that killed George Luckett and injured his wife had been fired from the same gun as that used in the killing of PC Haigh, it became obvious that a joint operation with the North Yorkshire force was required. The Home Office appointed Edward Griffith, Assistant Chief Constable of Nottinghamshire, to liaise with the Yorkshire force. Together with Detective Chief Superintendent John McNaught, head of Nottinghamshire CID, Edward Griffith travelled to North Yorkshire.

The day after George Luckett's murder, a brown 2.6 litre Rover saloon was seen parked at a holiday village on the Yorkshire coast. Its registration number – GYG 344T – checked out as the number of a 2.3 litre Rover owned by a company in Pickering. The difference in engine size seemed a minor factor, but when the police discovered that the real GYG 344T was still in Pickering, it became obvious that the car at the coast was using false plates. Officers returned to the holiday village, but the car had gone.

The search for George Luckett's stolen Rover came to an end at 6 pm, when the vehicle was spotted close to Dalby Forest by dog-handler PC Ken Oliver. Before PC Oliver had time to get his dog out from the rear of his van, a man emerged from the Rover, produced a handgun and began to shoot at him. Ken Oliver was hit in the arm by one shot, while another grazed his nose. As Ken took refuge in a nearby cottage, the gunman also fired at the police dog, but missed. Before running off into the forest of conifers, Ken's assailant set fire to the Rover car, and ripped the radio out of the police van.

Immediately, firearms experts from surrounding forces were brought in to help the local officers search the hundreds of acres of dense woodland. The police now revealed that they were looking for Barry Prudom, also known as Barry Edwards, a former soldier who had once been rejected as an SAS recruit because of his attitude to discipline. He had, however, received rigorous army training in survival methods, and had been using his undoubted skills to live rough on and off for almost eight years. Prudom, who had also worked on a North Sea oil rig and travelled abroad, was obviously a very dangerous man who had killed twice and who would not hesitate to kill again. His expert knowledge made him difficult to track down.

If Barry Prudom had stayed in the forest, living off vegetation and wild animals, he might well have evaded being seen for some time. However, on 28th June, hunger forced him to visit a post office shop in the village of Old Malton, a suburb on the outskirts of Malton. As Prudom came out of the shop, carrying bread and tinned food, he saw a police Panda car parked nearby. An unarmed police sergeant got out and came towards him. When a colleague inside the car shouted, 'Look out, Dave,' the sergeant dodged into an alley, but Prudom gave chase. He pursued the police officer over a wall and into a paddock, then caught up with him and shot him twice at point-blank range before running off towards the town centre. That night, the townspeople of Malton were warned to stay indoors behind locked doors, as armed police patrolled the streets and a police helicopter circled overhead.

Police Sergeant David Winter had been killed instantly, becoming Prudom's third murder victim. Winter, a 31 year old man with a wife and 14 month old daughter, helped to run a boys' club in Malton. A sergeant with the North Yorkshire police force, he had begun his police career in Nottinghamshire, working at Ruddington police station and at West Bridgford. PC Alan Thornhill, who had been best man at David's wedding, said later, 'He was a good friend and a very good policeman. We were cadets together. I was not surprised to hear of his bravery: he faced danger all the time as a police frogman and was always the type to have a go.' David's widow, Stephanie, said that her husband was devoted to his job and that his action in approaching Barry Prudom was typical of him. Despite her grief, Stephanie Winter spoke out against capital punishment and said that David had always been against a permanently armed police force.

Barry Prudom was now being described in newspaper headlines as a psychopath and a 'mad killer'. The police said that they had been seeking him in connection with a serious incident in Aldershot eight weeks earlier.

Mrs Shirley Roberts, a former girlfriend of Barry Prudom, described him as having a temper. 'It was not a quick temper,' she said, 'but when it started, it was terrible.' Barry Prudom's former wife had become very friendly with Peter Roberts,

Barry Prudom. (*Nottingham Post*)

Shirley's husband, while Barry was working in Saudi Arabia. When his wife had eventually gone off to Leeds to start a new life with Peter Roberts, Prudom had become obsessively jealous of his rival, describing in horrific detail all the things he would do to him. Shirley explained that Prudom believed that Peter Roberts was a former policeman, and she thought that this might well be the motive for him wanting to kill police officers. Shirley said that Barry had frequently boasted about the number of men he had beaten up in his past, and that before she had moved in with Prudom, he had admitted to her that he had a police record for violence.

The police confirmed that Prudom's ex-wife Gillian and his two teenage children were being guarded day and night at their home in Leeds. Gillian said that she was terrified in case Barry Prudom tried to contact her. She said that he had never forgiven her for standing up to him and walking out on their marriage, and had already threatened to kill her and her new husband. She described Prudom as moody, selfish and violent.

During June, there were 800 officers from 11 forces searching for the killer, although by 1st July the number had been scaled down to 200. Although the press carried reports that most of these men were fully armed, in fact only 16 officers – two teams of eight men – were carrying weapons.

At this stage the police brought in a man whose knowledge of evasion techniques was even more expert than Barry Prudom's, a tracker who the police hoped would lead them to their quarry. This was Eddie McGee, the author of *No Need to Die*, the book that Prudom had made his bible. It was now a case of the master survivalist hunting down his would-be disciple. Eddie McGee was not allowed to carry a firearm himself, but he was backed up by a team of eight officers armed with high-velocity rifles and handguns.

On 3rd July, Mrs Bessie Johnson of East Mount, Malton, went into her kitchen to unload the tea trolley, then took it into her dining room. Suddenly a man who had been hiding behind a chair came out to face her, saying, 'You know who I am, don't you?' Bessie replied that she was sorry but she didn't, at which the man produced a gun and marched her into the front room. He made her and her husband Maurice lie on their stomachs, and tied them up. Later, when he had eaten in their kitchen, he allowed them to sit down. Mrs Johnson told the gunman that her son Brian would be coming home, and asked that he be given the same chance as them.

The gunman – Barry Prudom – seemed to know everything about the Johnsons and their normal routine. He told them that he had been living in their outhouse for three days. Forty-five minutes later, 43 year old Brian Johnson returned home. Fortunately, when Brian saw his parents being held by the gunman, he ran into the house, where he too was taken prisoner and tied up. Prudom told Brian Johnson that if he had attempted to run away from the house, he would have received a bullet through his head.

During the period of their captivity, Barry Prudom told the Johnsons how he had killed Police Sergeant Winter and George Luckett. He said that after leaving the Lucketts' house to check how much petrol there was in their Rover, he returned to find George and Sylvia, who were still tied together by their elbows, holding a gun between them. Mrs Luckett was holding the butt of the gun and her husband was levelling the barrel, aiming it at him. He rushed at the couple and wrested the gun from them before shooting first George and then Sylvia in the head. Prudom claimed that he did not intend to kill Mrs Luckett. This version of events was called into doubt at the inquest into the death of George Luckett, when no evidence was found that Mr Luckett had fought back. The brutal truth was that both George and his wife had been shot in the head while sitting down.

Barry Prudom told the Johnsons that he wanted to kill more policemen, and that he had no intention of being taken alive. At 3 am the next day, after asking the Johnsons to give him a 24-hour start, he left and headed towards the nearby police station, where he could find many potential targets for his bullets. In fact, Prudom did not reach the police station; he found a derelict shed behind a wall at the town tennis courts and bowling green, and pulled a sheet of blue plastic over himself.

At 5 am, the Johnson family managed to free themselves. They had no idea whether Prudom was still watching their house, so they put on the upstairs light as if they were going up to bed; then Mr Johnson rang Malton police station to raise the alarm. The police immediately came to the house, accompanied by Eddie McGee.

The town of Malton was sealed off from the outside world. At 7 am, Eddie discovered a footprint in the Johnsons' garden, and two more prints in the dew-covered grass. Prudom, who throughout the murder hunt had been cleverly lying low during the daytime and moving about at night, had not on this occasion allowed for the heavy dew. It was to prove a fatal mistake. Eddie McGee went down on his stomach to check the dew-prints and was able to tell the police officers that the tracks were made less than an hour ago. 'As I looked ahead,' Eddie later recalled, 'some of the cobwebs were glistening, but there was one black piece which was not.' McGee followed the trail towards the tennis courts. There he crawled forward on his hands and knees until he saw a movement under the blue plastic sheet. 'I went forward,' said McGee, 'and I put out my hand. A foot hit me on the knee and sent me flying back.'

The foot belonged to Barry Prudom. The master tracker had found the man he had been seeking. His task complete, Eddie returned to the police station as the armed police officers with him took over, training their guns on Prudom's hideout.

Nearby householders were warned to stay indoors as the officers called out to Prudom, demanding his surrender. He refused to give himself up, and more armed police officers and a back-up squad were rushed to the scene. At 8.50 am, a number of shots were heard and the congregation at the nearby church were advised to stay inside. Further shots were heard at 9.07 am, and at 9.35 am the police fired two stun grenades into the hideout. More shots were heard at 9.46 am, and the police closed in and established that Barry Prudom was dead. At 10.30 am Chief Constable Kenneth Henshaw, who had directed the manhunt, confirmed Prudom's death and stated that the operation was over.

At the inquest into Barry Prudom's death, the jury heard that Prudom died on 4th July after being cornered at Malton tennis courts and bowling green. Dr Sava Savas, a Home Office pathologist, told the inquest that Prudom had two wounds to the head and 21 other injuries caused by pellets which had penetrated his body. One of the head wounds was from a .22 bullet and the other from a shotgun pellet. In his opinion, the wound caused by the .22 bullet was self-inflicted. This wound must have preceded the shotgun wound as either wound would have caused instantaneous unconsciousness or death. Forensic scientist John Burns told the jury that a bullet and cartridge case found by Prudom's body matched his Beretta pistol. The inquest jury returned a verdict that Prudom had killed himself.

During his 17-day killing spree, there were many rumours that Barry Prudom had at one time been a top-secret agent of some kind, involved in espionage. Although these stories were unsubstantiated, members of the Special Branch and an officer from the Royal Ulster Constabulary were present during or at the end of the manhunt.

Barry Prudom was buried in an unmarked grave at Harehill Cemetery in Leeds, after a funeral held in secret to keep away sightseers.

A year later, Eddie McGee was awarded a Certificate of Commendation for his bravery in leading police to the hideout of Barry Prudom. Chief Constable Kenneth Henshaw said, 'Mr McGee knew that should he find the wanted man, he would be in great danger.' The commendation was one of only eight provincial police awards for public acts of courage handed out in 1983 by the Association of Chief Police Officers.

9

DEATH
IN A PIGSTY

The Murder of William Straw at Burton Joyce
June 1985

In the early hours of Friday 21st June 1985, Nottingham police received a telephone call from Bulcote Farm, in Occupation Road, Burton Joyce. The caller, Mrs Norma Straw, told them that her husband William had collapsed in a pigsty and there were pigs milling around him. She was afraid to approach them and needed assistance. A police car was dispatched to the scene immediately.

When they arrived at the farm the police were faced with a macabre sight. A man was lying in the alleyway of a pig-pen, and six or seven excited pigs were rooting at him. The officers were forced to use their truncheons to beat off the pigs before they could examine the man. He was obviously dead, and they could see that he had been shot.

A post-mortem, conducted by Home Office pathologist Dr Stephen Jones, confirmed that the cause of death was a number of shotgun wounds. Dr Jones was able to rule out suicide, and a murder hunt was instigated immediately, led by Detective Chief Inspector Terry Cox, head of Nottinghamshire CID.

Bulcote Farm was actually a smallholding used for rearing pigs, rabbits, turkeys and bullocks. Its owner, 60 year old William Straw, had run an electrical business before taking up farming. A neighbour, Stanislaw Barszcz, who had been woken at 3 am on the Friday by all the police activity, described Mr Straw in the next day's *Nottingham Post* as a very clever and popular man. The same report said that Mrs Straw was being comforted by relatives in her large bungalow on the farm.

Bulcote Farm, Burton Joyce, where William Straw was shot dead in June 1985. (David Bell)

Police investigations were helped considerably when they received a call from a woman who had seen two men in a parked car only half a mile from Burton Joyce, on the night of the murder. The men were behaving suspiciously and covering their faces. To the delight of the police, this witness had noted the car's registration number.

By 24th June, the police had charged two 19 year old men – Philip Carney, of no fixed abode, and Jason Crisell, of First Avenue, Colwick – with the murder of William Straw. Significantly, Jason Crisell was William Straw's stepson. Both men appeared before magistrates at Shire Hall, Nottingham, and were remanded in prison custody.

The inquest into Mr Straw's death was held on 25th June; the coroner was Mr John Langham. Mrs Norma Straw told the inquest jury that late on the Thursday night, she and her husband had gone outside after hearing the pigs moving about the farmyard. She returned to the house, leaving William to put the escaped pigs back into the sty. When he had failed to return by 12.55 am, she went out again to look for him. She searched the outbuildings, using a torch as all the lights were off, and found her husband's body lying in the sty with pigs all around it.

Dr Stephen Jones reported that at the post-mortem, he had found three gunshot wounds, two to the body and one to the head. Any one of the three wounds could have been the cause of William Straw's death. The coroner then adjourned the inquest, 'pending the outcome of criminal proceedings'.

Events took a dramatic turn in November, when Norma Straw appeared in court, accused of the murder of her husband. She also faced a second charge that, between 1st May and 21st June, she had conspired with others to murder him. Detective Chief Inspector Bruce Foster told the court that two young men had already been committed for trial, charged with the murder of William Straw. Through her counsel, Mr Richard Nelson, Norma Straw made an application for bail, and after a 45-minute hearing, her application was granted; she was remanded on bail until 10th December.

The trial of Norma Straw and Philip Carney took place at Nottingham High Court in June 1986, before Mr Justice Tucker. The prosecuting counsel, Mr Brian Appleby QC, told the court that Norma Straw had plotted with her son and another man to murder her husband. Counsel further alleged that a plan for the two young men to gun down Mr Straw and then concoct an alibi for themselves was first suggested by Mrs Straw. The conspiracy had been hatched in the kitchen of the home of her adopted daughter, Lana Philpott, who overheard what was being planned.

The jury was informed that Jason Crisell, who was Norma Straw's son from a previous marriage, had already pleaded guilty to a charge of manslaughter on the grounds of diminished responsibility. He was now at Rampton high-security mental hospital.

The prosecuting counsel described how, after divorcing her first husband, Mrs Straw had left Wales and come to Nottinghamshire where she became William Straw's housekeeper and then his wife. Jason Crisell came with her, but went back to live with his father for a time before returning to Burton Joyce to live at the farm. Philip Carney was an old friend of Jason's, and their friendship was resumed around that time. Jason and his mother were devoted to each other but, over the years, serious conflict developed between Jason and his stepfather. Norma Straw always sided with her son.

By June 1985, William Straw was taking steps to have Jason evicted from Bulcote Farm. Jason finally left the farm on 14th June, taking his belongings with him, in circumstances of considerable anger. It was then that the conspiracy to kill Mr Straw took place. Carney and Crisell went to Wales, but on the evening of 19th June, they drove back to Nottinghamshire. They parked their car at Lambley, and walked half a mile across fields to the farm carrying a .410 single-barrelled shotgun.

The two men lured the farmer from his bed by disturbing his pigs. When he came down to investigate, Jason shot him, then reloaded and shot him again. He reloaded a third time, and passed the gun to Philip Carney who shot the farmer once more, at point-blank range. The two killers went to a phone-box and rang Norma Straw to tell her that her husband was dead. They then got into their Datsun car and drove away.

Although the call was made before 11 pm, Norma Straw waited over two hours before phoning the police. Her story that her husband appeared to have collapsed in a sty and that she was afraid to approach because the pigs were in an excited state was flawed in two respects, Mr Appleby alleged. First, it was inconceivable that the farmer's wife was genuinely afraid of the pigs, and second, she had rung for the police rather than the ambulance service. The reason for the delay, the prosecution continued, was to enable Jason Crisell and Philip Carney to return to Wales and establish their alibi.

A witness had observed the two men acting suspiciously in their car at Lambley, and had reported the details – including the car's registration number – to the police. Crisell and Carney were arrested in Wales.

Mrs Lana Philpott, Mrs Straw's adopted daughter, now said that statements she had given to the police, alleging that she had overheard her mother plotting with Crisell and Carney to kill William Straw, were untrue. She had signed them only because the police, during questioning, had threatened to include her in the murder charge and to have her baby taken into care. She did agree that her mother had complained some weeks earlier that Straw was trying to poison both her and Jason. Lana Philpott also claimed that a 16 year old girl who lived with her and who was 'possessed' by William Straw, had confessed that he had once asked her to poison Lana.

The prosecutor informed the court that Mrs Straw had told the police that she wanted her husband dead because he was a beast. She alleged he had committed 'acts of bestiality' on the farm and she had planned to divorce him.

Dr Stephen Jones told the court that William Straw had been standing up when he received the first gunshot wound, which was to his head. He was alive when all three wounds were inflicted, so any one of them could have been the cause of death. Dr Jones said that the dead man's clothing was disarrayed, but this was compatible with pigs rooting at the body.

PC Keith Spencer said that he went to the farm after receiving a 999 call from Norma Straw. PC Stephen Holloway said that when he returned to Bulcote Farm at 2.20 am to ask Mrs Straw about firearms, she suddenly said to him, 'I hope this is not a suspicious death.' He found this strange, as it had nothing to do with the conversation they were having. He added that Norma Straw seemed quite calm, and he could see no signs of distress.

Inspector Keith Beilby gave evidence that Philip Carney had made a voluntary statement to detectives that he had fired the third shot at Mr Straw as he lay dying from two shotgun wounds inflicted by his stepson. He claimed that Jason had promised him a job on the farm when he took over from his stepfather. In earlier interviews with the police, Carney had denied any hand in the killing, saying that he didn't think his friend would 'have the bottle' to commit murder. He later admitted that they had been planning the killing for several weeks.

Detective Superintendent Philip Newton said that he had interviewed Norma Straw at Hucknall police station in October, about four months after the murder. He asked her if she could remember saying that her husband had committed acts of bestiality on the farm. Mrs Straw had replied, 'Yes, he was a beast. Even the neighbours knew about that.' In a subsequent interview he had shown Mrs Straw a statement signed by her daughter, Lana Philpott, alleging that Mrs Straw was fully involved in a plot to kill her husband. Confronted with this she had put her head in her hands and said, 'Yes, he drove us to it.' Later she withdrew this admission, and refused to sign any statements. Detective Superintendent Newton added that Norma Straw denied being a dominating individual who had persuaded her son and his friend to kill her husband, so that she could inherit the farm.

Philip Carney told the court that he and Jason Crisell had returned to Nottingham on 20th June from a camping holiday in Wales. Jason had said that he was going to cause his stepfather aggravation by letting the pigs out. The two of them had crossed the fields to the back of the farm, carrying two shotguns, a 12 bore and a .410. After letting the pigs out, they had gone up to the flat above the pighouse, where Jason had once lived. Jason went down to frighten Mr Straw. Carney said that he 'froze with fright' when he heard the two shots. 'Until I heard that first shot, I had no idea that Jason meant to shoot Bill Straw,' Carney claimed. He ran down the stairs and saw Jason standing in the pigsty. He was pointing the gun down at Mr Straw, who was lying on the floor. Jason then fired the third shot into his stepfather.

Carney told the court that when he was questioned by Detective Chief Inspector Bruce Foster, he was told that if he co-operated he would face a reduced charge. 'He said he would get me two or three years instead of life,' Carney claimed. 'Mr Foster kept saying that I was guilty in law just by being there.' Philip Carney said he had agreed to confirm a statement that he had fired the third shot into Mr Straw, but said that he had only done so because Mr Foster had told him that it did not matter who had fired the third shot, because the victim was already dead. However, when, four months later, he asked about a reduced charge, the officer told him that it was out of his hands; the Director of Public Prosecutions had blocked the reduced charge when it became known that there was a third party involved.

Cross-examined by Brian Appleby QC, for the Crown, Philip Carney denied taking part in the killing because of greed. It was untrue that his friendship with Jason turned to greed when he was promised a job, a car and money when Jason inherited the farm. 'That was just empty talk,' he said.

Norma Straw said in evidence that there was no truth whatsoever in police allegations that she had persuaded her son and his friend to kill her husband so she could inherit his wealth. She had known for some weeks before his death that he owed £60,000 in debts. Within two weeks of her husband's death, the bank had sold all the stock and machinery, leaving 'not even a lawnmower'. Far from benefiting from William Straw's death, she was much worse off, and was now living on £33.99 a week social security.

She told the court that after two failed marriages, the first when she was just 18, she answered an advertisement placed by William Straw in 1979 in a newspaper circulating in north Wales. Bringing her son Jason with her, she became Mr Straw's housekeeper. They married two years later in 1981. She invested her divorce settlement, worth 'tens of thousands of pounds', in his farm. At the time of his death, the relationship was getting worse and she was making inquiries for a good solicitor to handle a divorce. Her husband was a very cold sort of person who showed no affection for her. On the night of 20th June, she was watching the television at about 10.30 when she discovered that the pigs had got out. She helped William get them back into the pen, then went out of the shed to see if there were any more outside, leaving her husband still inside the farm building. He had said that he might go down to the mill, so she went back into the bungalow. When he had not returned two and a half hours later, she went to look for him, intending to 'have a moan' about him staying out so long. She saw him, still alive, on the floor of the pig-pen with pigs all around him. She did not try to drive them off because she thought that someone might have hit him over the head, and that same person might attack her too. She was heartbroken when she heard that her son Jason had been taken into custody, charged with her husband's murder.

Summing up, the prosecution told the jury of eight women and four men that hatred and greed were the motives for the killing of William Straw.

Norma Straw's defence counsel, Mr William Andreae-Jones, conceded that there was clear evidence of matrimonial discord between his client and her husband. Although Mrs Straw might have been considering divorce, she still carried out her wifely duties, including washing her husband when he took a bath on the night of his death.

For Philip Carney, Mr John Devy QC said that because medical evidence had revealed that Jason Crisell had an abnormality of mind, he was guilty only of manslaughter. Philip Carney was before them because, although he had heard so many times Jason's threats to 'do in' Bill Straw, he – like everyone else – had not believed them.

Directing the jury, the judge said that if they believed Carney's account was untrue and thought that he was part of the killing, they should find him guilty of murder. If they thought his words were true, then they should consider a verdict of the lesser offence of manslaughter. The jury retired and took four and a half hours to reach their unanimous verdicts that Norma Straw and Philip Carney were both guilty of murder. Both were sentenced to imprisonment for life.

Following the trial, in October 1986, Mrs Wendy Hardy, the witness who had spotted Crisell and Carney behaving suspiciously in their car on the night of the murder and had noted the car registration number, attended a ceremony at Sherwood Lodge police headquarters. There she was presented with a Community Award by Mr Charles MacLachlan, the Chief Constable of Nottinghamshire.

Norma Straw sought leave to appeal against her conviction, but this was turned down by three appeal court judges. In a statement issued in June 1987, Lord Justice O'Connor, Mr Justice Davies and Mr Justice Schiemann said that medical evidence had indicated that Norma Straw was suffering from paranoid schizophrenia and the Crown had been prepared to accept a plea similar to that entered by Jason Crisell. However, Mrs Straw had flatly refused to enter such a plea and told her lawyers to fight for a complete acquittal. She had been told how she stood and was capable of deciding how her case should be put. On those facts, it was not permissible for her now to seek to change her mind.

10

A
GUILTY SECRET

The Murder of Karen Waters at Southwell
October 1985

In 1985, Karen Waters was a happy 17 year old, living and working in Southwell, an attractive small town with a beautiful cathedral, Southwell Minster. She worked at the New Minster Water Gardens and Garden Centre and lived with her boyfriend Adam Evison in a flat in Church Street.

Philip Wright also worked at the garden centre, and despite the 15-year difference in their ages – Philip was a balding 32 – he and Karen Waters seemed to be friends. From time to time, Philip would visit Karen and Adam at their home. The three of them would sometimes go for a drink together in the Bramley Apple public house next door. For Philip, however, there was one big problem about the friendship with Karen: he had a terrible secret in his past – a secret that would disgust people – and Karen knew all about it. He was never quite sure that she would keep this disturbing knowledge to herself.

Tuesday 29th October was Karen's day off, and she had decided to go shopping. She had accepted a lift with Philip, who had to go to Skegby for his employers. In Skegby, she did her shopping, then went with Philip for a pub lunch before returning to Southwell, where she was dropped off at her flat.

When Adam Evison came home from work just after 5.30 that evening, he entered the flat and, to his horror, found Karen's dead body lying on the floor, partially covered with a blanket. He rushed round to the pub next door, and the landlady Barbara Allen sent for the emergency services. Karen appeared to have

The Bramley Apple pub in Southwell, where Karen Waters, Adam Evison and Philip Wright used to drink. Karen and Adam lived in the flats next door. (David Bell)

been strangled, but she also had stab wounds to the chest, and her clothes were disarranged. The police set up a temporary incident room at the Bramley Apple.

At the post-mortem, Home Office pathologist Dr Stephen Jones found that Karen Waters's death was caused by asphyxia due to a ligature round her neck, and stabbing injuries to the chest. The police had no difficulty in finding their prime suspect because, like Karen, they knew all about Philip Wright's secret past: in 1984 he had been convicted of raping a 17 year old girl. After an evening out with the girl and her boyfriend, they had dropped the boyfriend off at his house, then Wright had persuaded her to drive him to an empty house where he had been doing some plastering work. Once there he asked her to help him collect some tools. Suddenly he attacked the girl, knocking her to the ground and squeezing her neck until she passed out. When she regained consciousness, Wright raped her, enforcing her acquiescence with threats of strangulation. For that crime he had been sentenced to three years' imprisonment, but had been released on parole licence after serving seven months.

It was not surprising, therefore, that the police would want to question Philip Wright about the events of Tuesday 29th October. The detective heading the inquiry into the murder of Karen Waters, Detective Superintendent Bob Davy, announced the next day that a 32 year old man was being interviewed in connection with the murder. On 31st October Philip Wright appeared before Newark magistrates, charged with Karen's murder, and was remanded in police custody.

His trial took place at Nottingham High Court in January 1986, before Mr Justice Tucker. Mr Andrew Jones QC, the prosecuting counsel, told the court that Karen Waters had lived with her fiancé, Adam Evison, a farm labourer. She worked as a café assistant at the New Minster Water Gardens, Southwell, where the defendant also worked. The prosecution alleged that Philip Wright was physically attracted to the girl, and became a casual acquaintance of the couple. He described how, on the day of her death, Wright had given Karen a lift to Skegby, and brought her back to Southwell, dropping her off at her flat. The prosecution alleged that Wright subsequently returned to Karen's flat and the killing occurred. The court was informed that the pathologist's report described blows to the head, strangulation, and at least seven stab wounds to the chest. The report concluded: 'It is probable that she had been rendered unconscious by strangulation with a ligature and was finally killed by the stabbing injuries.'

The prosecuting counsel continued, stating that when taken to Newark police station that evening, Philip Wright initially claimed that he had simply dropped Karen at her flat. Later, however, he broke down in tears and told the police: 'When I went back, she brought it up about the rape. I honestly don't know. I took my tie off and pulled.' In a subsequent interview, Wright claimed that Karen had threatened to report the rape conviction to his employers. He told the police that he had strangled Karen with his tie until she dropped, then interfered with her clothing and stabbed her with a work knife. The police later recovered the knife, which had a six-inch blade, from the garden centre.

Mr John Milmo QC, the defence counsel, said that there was no suggestion of any intention on the part of the defendant, when he called on the girl that day, to commit any offence, whether of rape or of murder. Something was said to him whereby he thought that his past was going to be made public, and it was in that moment of blind panic that he killed her. The tragedy was, the defence concluded, that there was something in Philip Wright which needed treatment and was probably treatable.

The jury brought in a verdict of guilty, and Mr Justice Tucker told Philip Wright, 'You were determined to kill her. You strangled her and then you stabbed her seven times. It was a senseless and a brutal offence, and as a result a young life has been taken.' He sentenced Wright to life imprisonment.

11

LIKE
A FIRE THAT DESTROYS

The Killing of Lynne Goldingay at Cinderhill, Nottingham

March 1985

Lynne Goldingay was born in Nottingham and educated at Frank Wheldon Comprehensive School in Carlton and at Digby College, where she took a two-year secretarial course. She went to D. W. Phipp & Co, a firm of accountants, as a temporary secretary until she was offered a full-time post there. Lynne met local celebrity Graham Neale at a pop concert, and soon started going out with him.

Graham had worked for the Post Office in Nottingham before becoming an engineer. In his spare time, he wrote reviews of bands and interviewed pop stars for the national music paper, *Sounds*. After working at Radio Nottingham as a sound engineer, Graham went to London and worked on *Rock On* on BBC Radio 1, with regular Saturday afternoon on-air spots interviewing music personalities. He returned to Nottingham and joined the independent radio station Radio Trent, where he set up *Castle Rockshow*, the only nightly independent radio rock show outside London. At this time, life could not have been sweeter for Graham. He had a fantastic job as a radio DJ, with his own shows on two local independent radio stations in the East Midlands. Besides the *Castle Rockshow* on Radio Trent, he also presented the *Graham Neale Rockshow* on Leicester Sound. At 31, he was a rising star, a somebody on the local music scene. He owned a bungalow in Brancaster Close in the Cinderhill district of Nottingham, and when, in 1981, Lynne agreed to move in with him, life was terrific. Lynne even took a part-time evening job as a receptionist at Radio Trent, where

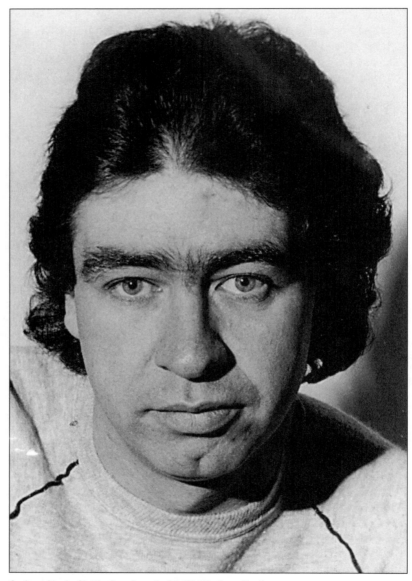

Graham Neale, Nottingham's radio DJ. (*Nottingham Post*)

Graham worked, so that she could be with him.

However, early in 1985, Lynne told Graham that she had been getting close to someone at the firm where she worked, and she needed time to think things over. She moved out, and went to live with her parents in Hickling Road, Mapperley. Eight weeks later, to Graham's delight and relief, she seemed to have made up her mind and returned to live with him.

Then, on Tuesday 27th March, Lynne disappeared. She failed to arrive at her place of work, and when her employer rang to see what was wrong, Graham said that she had set out for work at 8.30 am as usual. The police were called in, and the next morning they were interviewing hundreds of bus passengers as they travelled into Nottingham, showing them Lynne's photograph and asking if they had seen her on Tuesday morning. Her description – she was five feet one inch tall with blonde, shoulder-length hair – was circulated to police forces throughout Britain. Detectives also commenced door-to-door inquiries in Cinderhill.

Lynne's parents were baffled. Mr Lionel Goldingay said that his daughter would never have gone off without saying a word, or at least letting them know where they could reach her.

Graham Neale said that when Lynne had come back to him on the Saturday, they had had a marvellous time. On the Monday night they had gone together to a concert by Paul Young, a singer whom Graham had helped in his early days. Graham said that Lynne seemed happy that night, and he thought that the crisis in their relationship was over. She seemed quite normal as she left for work on Tuesday, but he had not seen anything of her since then. She had not taken any clothes or luggage with her when she left.

Detectives, led by Detective Superintendent Bob Davy, continued to question Graham Neale at Hucknall police station. Then, suddenly, a convoy of police vehicles – one of which contained Graham Neale – was seen setting out for Ratcliffe-on-Soar in the south of the county. There police found Lynne's body buried in a shallow grave in woodlands next to the power station.

Neale had broken down and confessed to the police that he had killed Lynne. On the way back from the Paul Young concert, in the early hours of Tuesday morning, their car had broken

The body of Lynne Goldingay was found in a shallow grave in woodlands by Ratcliffe-on-Soar power station. (David Bell)

down. By the time they got home Lynne had been in a bad temper, and in bed she had turned on Neale, taunting him about his sexual prowess. She had told him that there was only one man in her life, and it wasn't him. Neale claimed that he had completely lost control. Picking up a hammer that had been left in the bedroom because he had been repairing a light-fitting earlier, he battered her about the head in a blind fury, stopping only when he realised she was dead. The next evening, he had wrapped Lynne's body in a mattress and driven south, down the M1. Finding a secluded spot, he had dug a shallow grave and tried to conceal the body before returning home.

Graham Neale was immediately charged with the murder of Lynne Goldingay. As the news swept through Nottingham and Leicester, the many young fans who listened to his radio rock shows were amazed and devastated. Mr Ron Coles, managing director of Radio Trent and Leicester Sound, expressed his feeling of shock.

On 1st April, still wearing his usual leather jacket and blue denims, Neale appeared before magistrates at Nottingham's

Guildhall, and was remanded in custody. His solicitor, David Donaghan, told the court that Neale had asked to be absent from the next remand hearing on 10th April. The magistrates agreed, and also granted him legal aid. At a later hearing, Neale attempted to regain his freedom while awaiting trial by offering sureties of £20,000. However, bail was refused and he was again remanded in custody.

Lynne Goldingay's inquest was opened on 3rd April, before coroner Mr Peter Jenkin-Jones. Home Office pathologist Dr Stephen Jones told the court that he had unearthed the body in the presence of police officers, in woodlands near a lane leading to Ratcliffe-on-Soar power station. The cause of death was subdural haemorrhage associated with blows to the head. The body had been identified by Lynne's brother, Robert Goldingay. The inquest was then adjourned, pending the outcome of criminal proceedings.

The story took a new, tragic turn when on 29th May the body of a young man was found inside his fume-filled car in a garage in Gregory Boulevard, near the offices of the accountancy firm where Lynne Goldingay had worked. The dead man was Duncan McCracken, the 20 year old son of a Nottingham doctor. Duncan had been studying accountancy at Trent Polytechnic, and was on a one-year work experience contract at the firm where Lynne worked. He had fallen in love with Lynne – he was the work colleague about whom Lynne had told Neale – and had been devastated by her death. On 29th May he had gone back to the office, which was closed for the Spring Bank holiday. When his body was found in his car, he was surrounded by albums of personal photographs, and a notebook in which he had written a letter explaining that he could no longer live without the girl he loved.

An inquest into Duncan McCracken's death heard that his body had contained a lethal monoxide saturation level of 71 per cent. Dr James McCracken told the court that his son had suffered from extreme depression due to the death of his girlfriend. The court was told that Duncan had tortured himself by visiting alone all the places that he and Lynne had previously visited together. The coroner, Peter Jenkin-Jones, said that Duncan's was a tragic death because of the background circumstances, though they were not the direct concern of that court. He returned a verdict that Duncan had taken his own life by monoxide poisoning while acutely depressed.

Mrs Eunice Goldingay, Lynne's mother, who was still recovering from the shock of her daughter's death two months earlier, said, 'We were told straight away of Duncan's death. It has knocked us for six again. They had known each other since last November and Lynne seemed very happy.'

So far the story has included two deaths, that of Lynne, the murder victim, and of Duncan, her grief-stricken boyfriend, driven to suicide by the thought of life without her. But the list is still incomplete. Graham Neale, whose jealousy had started off the chain of events, was being held in Lincoln Prison, awaiting trial. When officers opened his cell on the morning of 6th June, they found his body hanging behind the door. He was taken down and certified dead at 7.20 am.

The reaction among his colleagues was mixed. Paul Mason, manager at the nightclub Rock City in Nottingham, paid tribute to the support that Graham had given to the music scene in the city, and said that he was stunned by the news of his death. John Hobson, acting station manager at Radio Nottingham, said that Graham's many friends were very shocked and upset. However, not everyone was totally surprised at the new turn of events. Dale Winton, who had once had his own show on Radio Trent, said, 'I wasn't as shocked as I thought I would have been when I heard about Graham's death, because of the culmination of events. Lynne was beautiful, she was lovely. I couldn't believe he could have done something like that.'

The inquest into Graham Neale's death took place in Lincoln. The coroner, Mr Humphrey Butcher, stated, 'All prisoners on remand on murder charges are taken into the hospital wing – in Lincoln it is automatic.' The principal prison officer, Mr Derek Parker, told the inquest that Neale's body was found hanging in his cell in the prison hospital wing. He said, 'I was approached by the hospital senior officer who informed me that he had found Graham Neale in his room on the second-floor landing, hanging behind the cell door. I went up to investigate and ordered him to be taken down.' Mr Parker stated that he arranged for the senior medical officer to examine Neale.

Pathologist Dr Bob Spencer told the court that death was due to hanging. He added that, in his opinion, it was consistent with having a twisted sheet drawn tightly around the neck.

Peter Holland, a fellow inmate of Graham Neale, told the inquest: 'He was thoroughly depressed about the whole situation. He was more depressed when he heard about the death of Mr McCracken. He thought it would lessen his chance of getting his own charge reduced to one of manslaughter. He said he could not cope with the thought of doing a life sentence, but never said anything about taking his own life.'

Coroner's officer Charles Hudson said that when Graham Neale was found, his feet were on the floor and his knees slightly bent. He described how Neale had meticulously made up his bed to make it look as though he were asleep. He added that Neale had left letters laid out neatly on a table, and these letters suggested that the writer was going to take his own life.

The jury returned a verdict of suicide. The coroner expressed sympathy to Graham Neale's mother, and also to the families of Lynne and Duncan. He stated, 'I would like to stress that Mr Neale was on a charge of murder and was not convicted. He had not been to court and therefore he was not guilty.'

One of Graham Neale's letters read:

> I'm quite sure that by many people I am regarded as some kind of nasty, cruel, insane animal or killer, now being responsible (although not directly) for the death of not one but two persons, namely my common-law wife/girlfriend Lynne Goldingay and her new partner Duncan McCracken. Whilst I am unable to give my side of the story as to how this tragic disaster occurred, I feel it only fair that someone should read this out at my inquest with the vain hope that at least a few open-minded people might then see me in a different light, and for what I was – namely a good honest citizen. I feel that most people will, quite naturally, assume that because Lynne decided to go and live with Duncan, I became outraged and therefore killed her. This is untrue. Please remember that my life at 30 was as good as it could ever have been. I had my perfect career, which I'd worked long and hard for, a nice home, friends and colleagues, and a tremendous girlfriend. All that I wouldn't just throw away, not to mention my freedom, if I didn't really love someone a great deal. I loved Lynne, and

still do. My guilt is not what happened to Lynne and Duncan, we all share that. My guilt is to another – I'm sorry, mum!

In a second letter, addressed to a friend, David Brett, Graham said that he was convinced that many of the facts of the case had been twisted or omitted.

Lynne, by her own decision, had returned to me on Saturday 23rd March, and stated that her relationship with Duncan was over. In fact, Lynne actually returned to her job at Trent, so they of all places should be well aware that she had returned. The implication at present is that we never got back together, which is totally untrue. Lynne was only seeing Duncan on a regular basis for some eight weeks (while away from the bungalow) and even during this time we went out socially, spoke each day, and exchanged birthday and Valentine cards. Lynne's relationship with Duncan was always described by her as 'casual' and had it been more than that it would have made no sense whatsoever for her to return home. If this new and short relationship was as serious as is now being suggested, then why did she take away her bungalow keys, never unpack her bags at her mother's home, never change her address, and want her Radio Trent job kept open? Basically, I was being as fair as possible by leaving her 'all doors open' and she took advantage of this. Hopefully, when, at the inquest, the true facts are reported, then my name might not be painted as black as it is at this present time. God bless you. Graham

Mrs Vera Neale, Graham's mother, said that when her son heard on the radio that Lynne's boyfriend had committed suicide, he thought that they were talking about him. As far as he knew, he was Lynne's boyfriend. That was the start of a depression which led to Graham taking his own life. He had no idea that Lynne was having a deep relationship with Duncan McCracken. She had never told Graham that she wanted to finish with him.

One person who did not accept Graham Neale's protestations that he still loved Lynne was Lionel Goldingay, who said: 'How can you kill someone you love that much? She had left Graham, gone back to him for a trial period, and she had informed him that she was leaving him again. She'd only been back with him for three days, but she realised that she was so much in love with Duncan. She was leaving Graham and was going to buy a maisonette with Duncan. I think that is the reason why he killed her. But you don't kill people you love. The end result is that three young people have just been wiped out. I don't think life for us – or for Duncan's family – will ever be the same again. How can you explain it? You can't. She was such a beautiful daughter.'

One factor which must have affected Lionel Goldingay was the knowledge that when he and his wife went to the bungalow on the Tuesday, Graham had assured them that Lynne had set off for work that day as normal, when in fact her dead body must have been lying only yards away in the house. The police described Neale's actions that day – he had also gone off to work where he behaved as though nothing had happened – as very callous.

The inquest into Lynne's death was resumed on 19th June. Dr Stephen Jones revealed that she had suffered five blows to the head from a blunt instrument, three of them serious and causing deep cuts to the skull. She also had superficial bruising to the neck which suggested that there had been a general struggle. Cuts to her hands and arms were caused as she fended off the blows and were of a type known as defence injuries. Detective Superintendent Philip Newton told the court, 'Criminal proceedings have now ended because the person charged with the murder of Miss Goldingay took his own life at 7.10 am while on remand in Lincoln Prison.' The coroner, Mr John Langham, recorded a verdict of unlawful killing.

The funerals of Lynne Goldingay and Graham Neale took place on the same day, a week after that of Duncan McCracken. At Graham's funeral, his favourite rock song – 'Music' by John Miles – was played. The Rev. Charles Knowles said, 'We must not let the tragic end to Graham's life make us forget to thank God for all that was good in his life and for those things we shall be happy to remember.'

Three hours earlier, at Lynne's funeral, the Rev. Richard More said that he believed love had consumed and in the end destroyed Lynne, Duncan McCracken and Graham Neale. He said, 'Love is like fire. Man depends on it, but when it gets out of control it becomes one of his deadliest enemies.'

12

THE
POLICEMAN AND THE TAXI DRIVER

The Death of Tom Ball in Nottingham
January 1990

Saturday night, for many people, is the high spot of the week. They go to the pub, to a show, to the pictures, they have a meal out, meet up with friends and generally enjoy themselves. Nottingham is no different from any other city in this respect. Saturday night means that the streets are full of people. For the police, it is the hardest night of the week. While a few drinks in the pub make some revellers happy, others become aggressive and are spoiling for a bit of bother. Taxi drivers view Saturday night with mixed emotions; it is a good earner for them but they are constantly aware that they could have trouble with customers who have been drinking. For 99 per cent of the time, the views of the police officer and the taxi driver will coincide.

However, the events of the night of Saturday 10th November 1990 were seen very differently by these two groups. The first the public knew of the incident was a report in Monday's *Nottingham Post* that a young policeman was critically ill in the Queen's Medical Centre. PC Tom Ball had undergone two emergency operations after suffering multiple injuries, including a fractured skull, in a traffic accident in the city centre. The 23 year old police officer had been off duty at the time, and had been on foot when he had been in collision with a taxi. This had occurred at 1.27 am in Lower Parliament Street. The police appealed for witnesses, particularly a woman who had been attending to the injured officer when the ambulance arrived.

Tom Ball never recovered. His death was described by

Superintendent Nigel Spencer, the subdivisional commander at Arnold, as a real tragedy; he added: 'He was a good experienced young officer who was showing great promise. His death has come as a shock to everyone.'

Tom Ball had joined the police as a cadet in 1983, becoming a constable three years later. He was first posted to Sutton-in-Ashfield, where he was described as quiet but very popular, with a number of close friends on the force. Tom transferred to uniformed duties at Arnold in 1988, and had begun a temporary attachment to the Central Vice Squad a week before his death. He was unmarried but had a steady girlfriend. His mother, Mrs Lydia Ball, was a member of Broxtowe District Council.

An inquest held before coroner Peter Jenkin-Jones on 15th November heard that Tom Ball had died from lacerations and bruising to the brain, following a collision with a black and white taxi in the early hours of Sunday morning.

The day after the inquest, Azhar Mahmood, a 22 year old taxi driver from Lenton, appeared before Nottingham magistrates charged with the murder of Tom Ball. He was remanded in custody, although when he appeared at Nottingham Crown Court four months later he was released on conditional bail with £15,000 sureties.

The taxi driver's trial began at Leicester Crown Court in July 1991 before Mr Justice Owen. Stephen Coward QC, for the prosecution, opened by alleging that Azhar Mahmood had used his taxi as a deadly weapon, running over Tom Ball, then reversing over him. Tom Ball had been drinking with a friend, Simon Alexander, another off-duty police officer. The two friends had got in a taxi in Old Market Square. They had only travelled round the corner into Lower Parliament Street when Tom asked the driver to stop at a takeaway and wait while he went inside. The driver stopped but refused to wait, demanding a £1.30 fare. Annoyed at the charge for the short journey, and at the fact that the driver wouldn't wait while he bought a takeaway, Tom Ball became abusive. The two men got out and paid the driver. Simon remained on the pavement, but Tom went to the front of the taxi and banged on the bonnet. Witnesses to the incident then saw the taxi driver rev his engine, move forward and hit Tom Ball. The vehicle ran over Tom's chest, then reversed over him. At this point, Tom suffered a fractured skull. Witnesses disagreed on whether Tom Ball got up after this, or whether he remained on the ground.

Azhar Mahmood told the police that there had been a row about the fare, and that he had intended to do a U-turn and drive back the way he had come. He claimed that he hadn't seen Tom Ball and that the collision was an accident. The prosecution alleged that the taxi driver had known full well that Tom Ball was in front of the car. He had deliberately driven over him, knowing it would cause serious injury.

In evidence, Simon Alexander said that Tom had sworn at the taxi driver and made offensive signs with his arms as he was crossing the road to the takeaway. The taxi suddenly moved to the right, hitting Tom, then reversed over his body. Cross-examined by James Hunt QC, for the defence, Simon Alexander denied that Tom Ball was drunk at the time and that the two of them had jumped the queue at the taxi rank. He said that they were both in good spirits, but were not drunk or staggering. The court heard that forensic tests showed that Tom Ball had drunk at least seven pints of beer.

David Monteith, a passer-by who had seen the collision, said that he spoke to the driver, asking what had happened. Mahmood had replied, 'I didn't see him.' Another eyewitness, David Pearce, told the court that he had overheard Mahmood tell someone, 'He was giving me hassle.'

In a taped interview, Azhar Mahmood told Detective Chief Inspector Harry Shepherd, 'I looked in the mirror and looked over my shoulder. I was just about to turn right when he was in front of my car. I felt an impact. I looked back while I was turning, and when I hit something I stopped. I reversed back to be stationary where I was before. I didn't know what I hit really, and when I saw him I was shocked. I think it was just an accident.'

Taxi driver Eric Robinson, who saw the incident, told the court that it looked deliberate at the time, because Tom Ball was standing at the front of the car with his hands on the bonnet.

Azhar Mahmood said he was aware of Tom Ball in the road and that he was making a noise, but thought that he had enough room to turn round without hitting him. 'When I first looked forward,' he explained, 'he was quite a distance from me. I thought he was going to cross the road to the chip shop. I looked in the side door mirror and looked over my shoulder, and turned the car round. I felt a bump under the car, but I was not aware I had knocked him down. I would have seen him if I had looked forward. I should have seen him.' Mahmood admitted telling passers-by that Tom Ball had been giving him hassle, but denied attempting to hurt Ball because he was angry. He said passengers often disputed fares and got angry with drivers, especially at weekends.

The prosecution alleged that Mahmood had known what he was doing. The defence said that Azhar Mahmood admitted that it was his fault, but he was not charged with causing death by reckless driving. He was being charged with murder, but the ingredients of murder were not there. 'Ball was drunk, staggering,' the defence counsel claimed, 'one moment on the pavement, the next on the road. There is no proof the taxi went right over the body. The car rolled up onto the chest, then rolled back. It is a natural instinct to roll back off an obstacle, then check what it is. That's precisely what Mahmood did.'

In his summing up, Mr Justice Owen said, 'This is a desperately sad, and in many ways, a tragic case. It is a matter of greatest concern to the family of that young man, Mr Ball. But it is also desperately sad for this young man's family.' The judge indicated Azhar Mahmood. 'A man of previous good character finds himself here charged with the most serious offence it is possible to put against anyone. It is all a terrible waste of life, but that doesn't mean the man is guilty. Don't rely on your emotions – emotion is a very bad judge, so please put it out of your minds.'

The jury returned a verdict that Mahmood was not guilty of murder but was guilty of manslaughter. The judge commented, 'To drive at someone in the circumstances of that time was a very foolish and dangerous thing to do. I bear in mind that there was behaviour that was provocative. It is nowhere near as serious or as bad as if you had been found guilty of murder.' Azhar Mahmood was sentenced to six years in prison.

After the case Tom Ball's mother said that the sentence was the right one. 'You bring your children up, you protect them all their lives, and then someone tells you a car has been driven at them. You just don't do that and get away with it. All right, Tom went out with a friend and had a few drinks, but it is so wrong that he is now in his grave.'

Nottingham's taxi drivers, who had demonstrated with a slow-drive protest in the city centre when Mahmood was originally charged, reacted to the six-year sentence very differently from Mrs Ball. 'For a policeman to behave in that way is out of order,' said one cabbie. 'The police should have more manners and watch how they behave.' Another taxi driver commented, 'To Azhar, Ball was just another difficult customer on a Saturday night. If it happened to him, it could happen to any one of us. From our point of view, it was accidental. I thought he might have got a couple of years at most.'

The Court of Appeal had some sympathy with this point of view. In April 1992, Azhar Mahmood's sentence was halved, the appeal judges ruling that the original six-year sentence had been too severe.

The day after the Court of Appeal made its ruling, five young gymnasts due to take part in the Disabled Olympics received a grant of £400 for specialist coaching from the Tom Ball Trust, set up by the police in memory of their young colleague.

13

THE
ONE-LEGGED TRAINSPOTTER

The Murder of Julie Dart in Newark-on-Trent
July 1991

Julie Dart lived on the Gipton housing estate in Leeds. She was born Julie Hill, but her surname was changed to that of her stepfather when she was five years old. At school, Julie was described as a bright but uncommitted student, but she excelled at athletics, particularly the 800 and 1,500 metres, representing her school – Foxwood High – and was good enough to make the West Yorkshire team.

While she was still at school, she took a couple of part-time jobs. She worked as a cleaner at the home of Michael Walter and she also worked at the Grill and Griddle café, where she first met her boyfriend, Dominic Murray. She left school at 16, and a year later moved from home to live with Dominic. Their relationship was a stormy one; Dominic liked a drink and, when drunk, he could become violent. She moved back to live with her mother again, who by this time was on her own. Julie got on well with her mother, Lynn, and the two of them liked to go out socialising together. Everyone said that they seemed more like best friends than mother and daughter. Even when they had arguments, they were like rows between sisters.

Julie's greatest ambition was to become a physical training instructor in the army, and in December 1990 she called at the local army recruiting centre and applied to join the WRAC as a driver. Despite suffering from mild asthma, she passed her medical, though she had refrained from mentioning her claustrophobia. Her application was progressing well and she was due to take her final selection examination in June 1991.

However, just before that exam, the recruiting office was contacted by Michael Walter, Julie's former employer. He informed the office that while a schoolgirl, Julie had stolen a credit card from his home and used it to obtain over £500. He claimed that Julie had admitted liability for the theft and was paying off the debt, adding that he was now worried that if she joined the army, she might not repay the outstanding amount.

Sergeant Lesley Holt discussed this with Julie on 10th June and she denied any debt liability. She went on to take her final selection tests in Guildford and passed with flying colours. Sergeant Holt telephoned Mr Walter, who still insisted that Julie owed him money. Julie Dart continued to deny that she had stolen the money but stated that she would pay it somehow, so that her WRAC career could go ahead.

There was only one way she could think of to raise that amount. She would sell her body on the streets of Chapeltown, the red-light district of Leeds. She told her mother that she was working on an evening shift at Hazelton Laboratories, sterilising syringes. She had now resumed her relationship with Dominic Murray, and she told him a different story: she was working as an evening orderly at Leeds General Infirmary. In the meantime, Julie turned up in Chapeltown and asked the prostitutes there for advice on how much to charge clients and where to take them.

On Tuesday 9th July, Julie phoned her mother at work, telling her that she was off to work and she would get a taxi home. She said that she would be back before midnight and asked that, if Lynn went to bed earlier, she should leave the door unlocked. In fact, Lynn Dart stayed up all night, waiting in vain for her daughter to come home.

At 8.30 pm, Julie was on the corner of Spencer Place. She went for a drink with two other girls, and while in the pub, she rang Dominic, telling him she was phoning from work. She said that she would stay the night at her mother's, and see him the next day. The girls returned to Spencer Place, where Julie and one of her colleagues each picked up a client. Later, the two working girls spent the money they had just earned at a tandoori takeaway. When they got back to Spencer Place, the third girl had gone. Julie's companion – a girl she had known since school – stayed with her until 11 pm before calling it a night. Julie was last seen sitting on a wall on her own, sometime between 11 and

11.30 pm. It was soon after this that she was kidnapped by a man who drove her to Newark-on-Trent in Nottinghamshire.

On Friday 12th July, Dominic Murray received a strange and worrying letter written by Julie. It was addressed to him at his sister's house, where he often stayed, and had been posted in Huntingdon, Cambridgeshire, the previous day. It read:

> Hello Dominic, Help me please. I've been kidnapped and I am being held as a personal security until next Monday night. Please go and tell my mum straight away. Love you so much Dominic. Mum phone the police straight away and help me. Have not eaten anything but I have been offered food. Feeling a bit sick but I'm drinking two cups of tea per day. Mum – Dominic HELP ME. Dominic, my mum will be in at five every night. Or phone, yes phone her. 832600 EXT 3844. IF NOT WORKING GO TO HER HOUSE. Love you all, Julie.

A very concerned Dominic rang the number Julie had given. It was Lynn Dart's work number at Leeds Polytechnic. Lynn left work immediately and rushed round to his sister's house. She read the note, then made several phone calls to friends in an attempt to discover where Julie might be. When she failed to track her down, she took the note to the police.

The same day, by second post, the police received a typed ransom note also posted in Huntingdon at 7 pm on 11th July. It said that a young prostitute had been kidnapped from the Chapeltown area and demanded £145,000 for her release. The letter threatened that if things went wrong, not only would Julie disappear for ever, but a firebomb would be planted in a city-centre store, and then the whole operation would begin again with the kidnapping of an electricity, gas or water board employee in the course of their work.

Although some officers wondered if the whole thing might be a hoax, Detective Sergeant Bob Taylor had previously worked on the Yorkshire Ripper case, and this experience made him take the ransom letter seriously. His inquiries soon revealed Julie's double life. He worked out her movements up to her disappearance late on the night of Tuesday 9th July.

Bob Taylor returned to the ransom letter. The writer demanded £140,000 in cash with a further £5,000 in two bank accounts with cash cards, PIN numbers and a withdrawal limit of £200 per day. The cash was to be in used £50, £10 and £5 notes and wrapped in polythene, then in brown paper secured with nylon cord with a substantial loop at the top. The instructions went into considerable detail: there was a diagram of how the parcel should look, and a demand that the polythene inner wrapping should be 'at least 120 microns'. A policewoman was to go to New Street railway station in Birmingham at 7 pm on Tuesday 16th, and wait in a phone-box inside the platform 9 waiting room. She would be phoned with further instructions which would take her from phone-box to phone-box along country lanes, where the presence of any police vehicles or surveillance helicopters would be obvious. She would eventually be led to a location where a rope with a doglead clip was hanging from a tree. She was to attach the parcel of money, then return to the car. The young man who would collect the parcel would not be the kidnapper, but a young man from a car parked in a lovers' lane, whose girlfriend would be held hostage until the money was collected.

The next Tuesday, a female police officer was in the waiting room in New Street station, as the kidnapper had directed. At 7.06 pm the phone rang and she answered it, but the line went dead.

Meanwhile, the West Yorkshire police had interviewed Julie's friends and family. Initially suspicion fell on two men, her boyfriend Dominic Murray and her one-time employer Michael Walter. Dominic was easily ruled out, as he had a broken ankle set in plaster, making it impossible for him to drive a vehicle. The inquiries now centred on 41 year old bachelor Michael Walter. He could have had a motive connected with the stolen money, and his friendship with several teenage girls seemed strange, although he had never had a sexual relationship with any of them. The tough estate where Julie had lived was by now buzzing with the rumour that Michael Walter had killed her. The local pubs were alive with threats that her friends and neighbours would take the law into their own hands and 'sort him out'. Michael was taken into police custody for three days and nights, and his house was thoroughly searched. Even when he was released on Thursday 18th July, he was kept under 24-hour surveillance.

The next day, Lincolnshire farmer Bob Skelton intended to drive some of his cattle along an old railway cutting towards his farm at Easton, near Grantham. Together with his 18 year old son Andrew and his YTS employee Kevin Russell, he set out to wire the gates along the route so that the cattle could not stray into the fields. They had parked their Land Rover and lifted out the barbed wire when they saw a pink and white bundle under an oak tree in the corner of a field. Bob was not surprised. People were always using the area to dump their rubbish. The three men walked over to it and found that it was wrapped in a striped sheet and tied up with green rope. Andrew cut the rope, then sliced a hole in the sheet. There was an unpleasant smell and Bob thought he could see a human arm.

Leaving the younger men to guard the bundle, Bob drove back to his farm and called the police. When they arrived on the scene they found that the bundle contained the naked body of a young woman who had apparently been battered to death. Bizarrely, the woman's head was completely bald. Home Office pathologist Stephen Jones arrived at 11.30 am and made his first examination before the body was removed. From the lack of staining to the ground, the police established that the bundle could have been there for only a few hours.

The body was taken to Grantham and Kesteven Hospital for a full post-mortem. Dr Jones found that there were two fractures to the skull. The corresponding indentations to the back of the head had been caused by a heavy instrument such as a hammer. Also, at the back of the neck were marks caused by a ligature. He concluded that the woman had been rendered unconscious by the blows to the head, then strangled to death. There was no sign of any defence injuries to the arms or fingernails, indicating that she had not been able to put up a fight against her attacker. There was no sign of any food in her stomach, so she had not eaten for at least eight hours before her death. Decomposition prevented the pathologist from being able to discover whether she had been sexually assaulted. There was no indication that her wrists had been tied up, but there were chain-like marks on the right ankle. From the degree of decomposition, Dr Jones believed that the young woman had either been dead for several weeks, or the body had been kept in a warm environment. From the small amount of insect activity, it seemed that the body must have been kept in a sealed container until two days ago.

The Lincolnshire police sent out a telex to other forces, asking them to check their missing person files. In Leeds, Superintendent Taylor read the request and asked whether the dead woman had a chipped tooth. She had, and dental records quickly established that the body was that of Julie Dart. This was confirmed when Lynn Dart recognised Julie's wishbone ring, found on the middle finger of the dead girl.

One thing was certain: whoever had killed Julie, it could not have been Michael Walter, since he had been under police surveillance at the time the body was being dumped in Lincolnshire. The police now had to face the unwelcome fact that Julie had probably been chosen at random. The fact that her murderer was previously unknown to her would make the job of catching him much more difficult.

However, the killer wanted to stay in touch. On Monday 22nd July, the West Yorkshire police had another communication from him, written on the same typewriter as before. This letter had been posted at Leeds railway station on the Sunday, but its contents implied that it had been written a few days earlier. It read:

> Words will never be able to express my regret that Julie Dart had to be killed, but I did warn what would happen if anything went wrong. At the time of this letter there has been no publicity. If you do not find the body in a few days I will contact you as to the location. It will have to be moved today as it appears to be decomposing. She was not raped or sexually abused or harmed in any way until she met her end. She was tied up and hit a few blows to the back of the head to render her unconscious and then strangled. She never saw what was to happen, never felt no pain or knew anything about it. I still intend to carry out this campaign until I receive the monies however many people suffer. In two weeks or so I shall demonstrate my firebomb. I still require the same monies as before under the same conditions, if you want to avoid serious fire damage and any further prostitute's life.

The police followed the kidnapper's instructions by placing a message reading 'Let's try again, for Julie's sake' in the personal column of the *Sun* on the following Saturday. On Tuesday 30th July, the police had another letter, handwritten in block capitals this time, saying that the same policewoman used in the failed Birmingham delivery was to be at a named phone-box at Leicester Forest East services on the M1 that day at 8.30 pm. She would be given instructions to follow a trail that would eventually lead to a pick-up point. As with the earlier attempt, the cash would be collected by the male member of a courting couple, while the kidnapper was holding his girlfriend at gunpoint.

The police were at the location at the due time. The phone at Leicester Forest East rang, the policewoman picked it up, but the tape played to her was incomprehensible. When she said that she couldn't understand it, the line went dead.

The police received a fourth letter on 1st August, saying that the caller would ring the following Tuesday. This letter, again handwritten in capital letters, was posted in Coventry. The police waited at Leicester Forest East on that day, but received no call.

A fifth letter, postmarked Nottingham, was received on Friday 5th August. This communication was typewritten but on a different machine from that used for the first two letters. It explained that the writer had been unable to find a suitable prostitute to take hostage on the Monday night, and that the courting couple he intended to use to collect the cash were not there in the lovers' lane on Tuesday evenings. This couple, he added, 'are more important than the prostitute as a prostitute can be eliminated at any time should the police not co-operate'. The kidnapper wrote that the day would have to be changed to a Wednesday, and said he would ring 'the usual location' on Wednesday 14th August. Referring to Julie Dart's body, he said that the police had found it within 24 hours, adding, 'I did think of hiding her body till it was all over but felt sorry for her. She was only killed because she saw where she was.'

On 14th August the police were back at the M1 service station; this time the kidnapper did phone and the ransom trail began. The caller said that he had kidnapped a prostitute called Sarah Davies in Ipswich. After demanding the registration number of the female police officer's car, he directed her north up the M1 back into the West Yorkshire police's own territory. At 9.56 pm, the officer was to be at a named phone-box in Wakefield. She was there, but when she tried to pick up the receiver, it jammed in its cradle and communication was lost. The kidnapper had intended to send the officer from point to point, picking up written messages, but this part of the scheme went wrong.

In South Yorkshire, the police knew nothing of the West Yorkshire force's operation. When a South Yorkshire officer spotted a suspicious package beneath a bridge at the side of the motorway, he sent for the bomb disposal squad and had it blown up. A tin was destroyed, but what remained was a white brick with an envelope attached. The envelope had a figure 3 on it, and inside was a stencilled note which directed the finder to a footbridge over the M1, half a mile away. There the police found another white brick but nothing else. It didn't seem of any great interest to them, and they decided it was probably part of some children's game; it was the school holidays, after all. Another envelope, this time marked with a figure 2, was later found in a phone-box near Barnsley, and the note inside it proved to be part of the same ransom trail.

The West Yorkshire police concluded that the paperchase had been meant to lead them to the footbridge which carried the Dove Valley Trail over the M1. The officer would have been instructed to halt on the motorway and attach the ransom money to a rope suspended from the walk above.

This theory was confirmed when the police received a sixth letter from the kidnapper, postmarked Grantham, on 19th August. In it he said that he had aborted his plan when the South Yorkshire police had closed the M1 to carry out the controlled explosion on the suspect package. He said that he had not in fact kidnapped a prostitute in Ipswich. 'I didn't need to. Following Julie's death, you would co-operate in anything I wanted.' He also told the police 'for their records' that Julie's body had deteriorated so quickly because he had kept it inside a wheelie-bin for two very hot days. 'I thought this was the best way to keep the body. The head was wrapped in a towel, but when this was removed to clean her up . . . her hair came away, stuck to the blood on the towel. The wheelie-bin was used to transport the body to where you found her.'

A seventh letter from the kidnapper was received in October. In it, the killer told the police that they were nowhere near to catching him. As the sentence for two murders would be no greater than for one, he would kidnap another prostitute and kill her unless he was paid his £140,000. He instructed the same WPC to be at the phone-box on platform 3 of Carlisle station at 8 pm on 21st October. The writer denied that reported attacks on prostitutes in Bradford and Sheffield were his doing, stating that he would kill only for money, not for sex. He added primly, 'I wouldn't have sex with a prostitute.' He also revealed why his letters had such different postmarks: he had dropped the stamped, addressed letters on trains, relying on whoever found them to post them.

The police were at Carlisle station on the arranged date, but received no phone call.

After a failed attempt to extort £200,000 from British Rail by threatening to derail an Intercity express, Julie Dart's murderer returned to the notion of kidnapping. This time he would not take a prostitute, but someone whose employers might part with the ransom money.

Stephanie Slater worked as a sales negotiator at a branch of Shipways, a firm of estate agents owned by Royal Insurance. On Wednesday 22nd January 1992, her first appointment was to show a client called Bob Southall around an empty property in Turnberry Road, Great Barr, about a mile away from the office. Stephanie had not met Bob Southall before; she had not been in the office when he had called and spoken to Sylvia Baker, the office clerk, nor when he had collected the house details from her colleague Jane Cashman.

Stephanie drove to the appointment and parked outside. A man was already waiting by the front door, with a clipboard in his hand. Stephanie hurried towards him and asked, 'Mr Southall?' He muttered an affirmative reply; Stephanie apologised for being a few minutes late, and let the two of them in. Although 25 year old Stephanie had worked at Shipways for only five weeks, she had six years' previous experience with another firm, Connell's, and she was used to sorting out the genuine buyers from the time-wasters. Although he asked about double glazing and damp-courses Stephanie soon formed the impression that Bob Southall was not really interested in the property. She was not very surprised: the house was run down and would need a lot of money spending on it.

She took a closer look at the client, mentally summing him up.

He was in his forties or early fifties, about five feet eight inches tall, and wearing heavy-rimmed glasses. He had on a duffle coat with a picture of a train on the breast pocket, and he smelled slightly of industrial oil or grease. He wasn't dirty, just slightly grubby and fairly nondescript. From his perfunctory questions about the house, Stephanie could tell he had a soft northern accent.

When they were in the bathroom, the client pointed to a hook above the bath and asked Stephanie what it was. She stepped closer to take a look, but when she turned round she was terrified to see that he was holding a twelve-inch chisel in one hand, and a knife with a nine-inch blade in the other. The grubby little man seemed to have grown larger.

In a tone much louder and harsher than before, he snarled, 'All right!' The man clenched his teeth and moved forward. Stephanie struggled with him, receiving a cut to her hand. When the attacker put his hand over her mouth, she bit his finger, but he kept coming forward and pushed her into the bath. When she found the knife – a home-made weapon with a bandage where the handle should be – pressed against her throat, Stephanie decided that to fight on would be counterproductive. She remembered reading a book by Dr Miriam Stoppard, which advised women under attack not to panic or to cause the attacker to panic, but to remind the antagonist that he was dealing with another human being.

'All right, all right, calm down. You've got me,' she said. 'Remember I'm human. Please don't kill me.'

The man replied that no one was going to kill or harm her, and warned her to lie still. He produced a piece of washing line and tied her wrists together, before putting a pair of spectacles with thick, dark lenses onto her face. 'Get out of the bath,' he instructed. Stephanie struggled to obey, but the spectacles were too large and fell off. 'Don't look at me!' he shouted, snatching them up and putting them back on her. He produced another piece of washing line, which he tied into a noose and placed around Stephanie's neck. For one terrifying moment, she wondered if he planned to hang her in the empty house.

He told her that they were going downstairs, and with his hands on her shoulders, steered her down the stairs and told her to sit down. He tore up her scarf and used a piece to blindfold her. He placed some rough material in her mouth before gagging her. Finally, he tied her legs together loosely just below the knees.

Hardly able to walk, Stephanie was guided out through the french windows and down the garden to the garage. Her kidnapper told her that there was a car and she was to get into it. She climbed in the passenger seat, which was reclined at an angle that was almost horizontal. Her attacker fastened a rope under her chin, preventing her from leaning forward. Her face was covered with a lightweight blanket, and then what seemed to be a coat.

Finally, a heavy box – possibly a metal toolbox – was placed on her lap. The man pulled her coat to one side, and Stephanie felt the cold knife blade press against her stomach. After a threat that the knife would be used if she made any moves, the car moved off.

Stephanie made one small error of judgement at this time. When she complained that the coat over her face was preventing her from breathing, she was asked how she knew it was a coat. 'Because it feels like a coat,' she snapped sarcastically. The attacker replied, 'Oh, you're clever as well,' his sneering tone indicating that he was ruffled. Stephanie realised that she had broken her self-made vow to keep him calm, and resolved not to make the same mistake again.

After driving for some time, the car stopped and Stephanie formed the impression that they were in a large, empty car park. The kidnapper asked her for her name and told her that she was to call him Bob, though it wasn't his real name. He removed the heavy box from her lap, and told her that she had been kidnapped. Stephanie was amazed; her parents were not rich. However, her kidnapper informed her that she was to make a tape for him to send to Shipways, her employers.

Still unable to sit up, she had to turn her head and speak into a microphone, repeating the words she was instructed to say: 'This is Stephanie Slater. The time is now 11.45. I can assure you I'm okay and unharmed. Providing these instructions are carried out, I will be released on Friday 31st January. By Wednesday you will need an Ordnance Survey map 103 for Blackburn and Burnley. Kevin Watts must be the person that acts as courier and uses his car. Sylvia or Jane may be passengers to act as guide, but only these two people must be in the car. The passenger must never leave the car. Next Wednesday, at every point where instructions are given, the boot of the car must be opened for thirty seconds. Money must not be marked in any way whatsoever or contain any device whatsoever.'

When the message was completed, Bob put the tape into an envelope, instructing Stephanie to lick the gummed flap. The kidnapper obviously knew that the police scientists could obtain his DNA profile from a sample of his saliva. He informed his victim that he was leaving the car to post the tape and to make a phone call. It was not long before he returned, saying, 'That's that done. Kevin Watts will have that in the morning.' Stephanie realised that her kidnapper knew the name of her boss, as well as the names of her two colleagues; he had done his research thoroughly. She also remembered that in the dictated tape message Bob had mentioned releasing her on 31st January. She realised with a sinking feeling that he intended keeping her captive for more than a week.

They drove on for another hour, before stopping by the side of the road. Bob offered Stephanie a ham sandwich, which she refused. She did not tell him that she was a vegetarian in case it annoyed him. She agreed to accept a drink of tea and a piece of chocolate. Asked whether she needed to go to the toilet, she hastily refused, imagining what the procedure might involve. He told her that they still had a long journey in front of them, and warned her to forget any ideas about personal modesty, as he was going to be 'babysitting' her for eight days. Later on the journey, Stephanie had to ask him to stop as she had stomach ache, and had to endure the humiliation of Bob assisting her – still blindfolded and gagged – to use a field as a lavatory.

He told her that they had some time to kill, as he didn't want to arrive at their destination before dark. Just like Julie Dart, Stephanie Slater was heading for Newark-on-Trent.

When they arrived, the car drove down a bumpy track before coming to a halt. Stephanie heard a metal door being opened, then Bob returned to steer her – still bound – into a building with a stone or brick floor. She was allowed to sit on a wooden chair. Her ankles and wrists were fastened with handcuffs and she was roped to the chair. Bob left the building for 10–15 minutes to fetch some fish and chips; Stephanie forced herself to eat just five chips before being told to lie on a mattress. Bob removed her clothes and raped her; he then gave her a large pair of jeans and two jumpers to put on.

He said that he hoped she was not claustrophobic as she was going to sleep in a wooden box. Still blindfolded and gagged, Stephanie was forced to shuffle into a coffin-like, lidless box that was wedged inside a plastic wheelie-bin lying on its side. To fit in, Stephanie had to lie on her back with her hips and lower body twisted at an angle. Her wrists were handcuffed to a metal bar above her head. Bob told her that if she pulled on the bar, boulders would come down on top of her and crush her. He also said that an electric wire running the length of her box would give her a shock if she moved. Finally, he closed the wheelie-bin lid and bolted it, telling her that she would not suffocate as he had thoughtfully made air-holes in it. He then left the building.

Stephanie spent an agonising night. She was very cold, her back was protesting at its twisted position, and her arms were suspended above her head. Above all, she was alone with her thoughts, wondering what the future held for her.

The next day Bob returned and allowed Stephanie out of her box. He removed her gag, but left the blindfold in place. She was unable to use her arms at all, and Bob had to massage them before she was able even to pick up a cup of tea. Afterwards, Stephanie thanked him. Bob reacted strangely, seemingly angry about his victim expressing gratitude to him. Objectively he was right – Stephanie had absolutely nothing to thank him for – but on another level she had reminded the kidnapper that he was still dealing with a human being.

He became more compassionate, cooking some porridge for her, and agreeing to saw off part of her wooden 'coffin' so that she would be able to lie flat in it. He told her that if Shipways paid him £175,000 and if Stephanie behaved herself, there was no reason why she shouldn't be back with her parents the following week. Being careful to speak in the plural, he told her, 'We don't want to hurt you but we will if we have to.'

Stephanie spent her nights in the box inside the wheelie-bin, but in the daytime she was manacled to a chain long enough to reach the wooden chair, the mattress, and the bucket she had to use as a toilet. Bob left on a radio playing Radio 2 during the day, but Stephanie could also hear distant muffled voices and the occasional ring of a bell. It sounded like a shop door opening and closing, and she decided that the voices were those of customers. She thought she might be in a workshop behind a garage.

She held several conversations with her captor over the next few days, telling him about her life. Bob told her that he disapproved of pubs and of people marrying too young. He seemed distressed to learn that she was adopted. Although most of their conversations were friendly, Stephanie was horrified when Bob told her that he had decided to get rid of a wheelie-bin. This was not the one she was forced to sleep in, but one he said he had been keeping to take her body away, if she had disobeyed his instructions by removing her blindfold. Several times he referred to a 'mate', a man who was part of the kidnapping scheme. He said that his mate was 'a nasty piece of work' and told Stephanie that she was lucky that this other man wasn't looking after her. When Stephanie heard a motor bike, Bob told her that it belonged to his mate, and that he would be using it to pick up the ransom money.

Meanwhile, back in the outside world, Shipways had informed the police about Stephanie Slater's disappearance. A media blackout was enforced to prevent the kidnapper learning that the police had become involved. One line of inquiry was to see whether this event was linked with any others. The unsolved disappearance of estate agent Suzy Lamplugh in 1986 was one such, but the recent case of the kidnapping and murder of Julie Dart seemed more likely to be connected to the new case. The envelope that had contained the tape of Stephanie's voice also contained a typed ransom note demanding £175,000. The misspelling of the word ransom, written as 'ransome', and the repeated use of certain phrases, gave the police reason to believe that Julie Dart's murderer, the British Rail extortionist, and Stephanie Slater's kidnapper were one and the same. It was an alarming thought; Julie Dart had been murdered 48 hours after her kidnapping.

Shipways had been told to pay the ransom on Wednesday 29th January, a week after the kidnapping, with Kevin Watts as the courier. Kevin was determined to do all that he could to get his colleague released, and turned down an offer to replace him with a police officer of similar appearance. Royal Insurance, the owners of Shipways, arranged for £175,000 to be paid into a police account, and the ransom money was withdrawn in the denominations the kidnapper demanded. A thousand detectives from Midland forces were assembled into a squad to prepare for the ransom run. West Yorkshire officers from the Julie Dart case were invited to attend meetings but were not made part of the squad.

On the Wednesday, Kevin Watts went to work as usual. The police gave him a bullet-proof vest to wear, and at 2.30 pm a detective arrived with the ransom money in a blue sports bag. A tracking bug had been sewn into its base, and a two-way radio had been installed in Kevin's car. At 3.25 pm, 25 minutes late, the phone rang and the kidnapper told Kevin to drive to Glossop, in north-west Derbyshire. The chase was on.

As Kevin Watts headed north in his Rover, the kidnapper was leaving Glossop and making for West Yorkshire. He was once again going to a bridge over a former railway line, now known as the Dove Valley Trail. The spot he had chosen was where Blacker Green Lane passes under the Dove Valley Trail, close to the M1. He parked his car and got a Suzuki motor-scooter out of the back. Freezing fog was closing in as he made his final preparations.

Meanwhile Kevin's car chase had taken him to Glossop, then Barnsley, then Sheffield. He found his final message in a phone-box near Dodsworth and proceeded to drive to Blacker Green Lane. He was making slow progress because of the fog. The police were also having problems. The two-way radio in Kevin's car was not working properly; although the police could still hear Kevin repeating each message in his car, he could no longer hear them. In the open countryside they were reluctant to get too close in case the kidnapper heard the sound of their car engines, and the tracker bug in the sports bag was fading. Not that this mattered; the kidnapper had already made Kevin transfer the money into another bag.

Kevin Watts repeated aloud his last message from the kidnapper, hoping that the police could still hear him, then began to drive very slowly through the thick fog towards the pick-up point. A Shipways sign by the side of the track told him he was on the correct route. Suddenly he spotted a cone barring his way. There was a different message attached, telling him to ignore the last instruction as he now had 60 seconds to go to a wooden tray on a wall and put the bag onto it. The tray had a sensor to detect bugs; if the buzzer did not sound, Kevin was to return to his car, move the cone and drive on. Kevin Watts did as instructed.

Down on the Dove Valley Trail, 60 feet below, the kidnapper heard Kevin's car drive away. He tugged on the rope he had rigged up earlier, and the tray and its contents fell at his feet. He stuffed the money into the panniers of his motor-scooter and chugged off down the trail. Despite falling off the bike three times on the icy track, he reached his car and loaded the bike and the money into it, before driving back to Newark.

From the police viewpoint, the operation was a disaster. Communications were going haywire, men were rushing around, and when they found Kevin Watts and heard his account, they realised that they had lost the money, lost their man, and probably lost the kidnapped girl. Now the kidnapper had the ransom, he had no reason for keeping Stephanie alive.

In her prison, Stephanie was beginning to panic for the first time, wondering whether her captor would return. When she heard him enter the building, her chief emotion was a feeling of relief. 'Did everything go all right?' she asked him. 'Yes,' he replied, 'apart from my mate falling off his motorbike three times.' He ordered the girl to put on her own clothing, and led her to his car. She was not tied up this time, although she was still blindfolded. In the car Bob came out with the statement that he would be taking her to a spot near her home as he didn't want anyone 'getting hold of her'. The kidnapper, who had raped his captive on the first night of her imprisonment, seemed completely oblivious to the irony of his words.

Together they drove back to Birmingham, and as they got near to Stephanie's home she was allowed to take off her blindfold. Stephanie kept her eyes closed, anxious not to look at her captor and cause him to change his mind about letting her go. Stephanie was dropped off at the top of the road where she lived. Before he drove away, Bob said, 'None of this was your fault. Get back to your normal life as soon as possible. You may need counselling. I'm really sorry it had to be you.' He then demanded a goodbye kiss. After he had gone, Stephanie stumbled back to her home and was reunited with her parents. It was 12.50 am.

Stephanie Slater told the police about the coffin in the wheelie-bin and described what she could about the workshop where she had been kept. A female police surgeon took samples from her hair and, from beneath her finger and toe nails, and swabs from her hands and feet. She told no one that she had been raped, partly to spare her parents' feelings but also because she wondered whether the fact that she had not resisted might make the charge of rape somehow invalid. In addition, she felt that she could not endure the intimate examination that would ensue. She could not wait to get into a hot bath and wash away the grime of the past week.

Two days after losing the £175,000 ransom money, the West Midlands force lost control of the inquiry. Tom Cook, Assistant Chief Constable of West Yorkshire, was appointed head of the joint Julie Dart/Stephanie Slater inquiry. It was another three days before the computers of the West Midlands and West Yorkshire police forces could be made compatible enough to exchange data.

Julie Dart's family were pleased when they heard that there was now a joint operation into the two cases. Dominic Murray said that he thought the murderer would now be caught.

Artist Julia Quenzler was brought in to draw a likeness of Stephanie's abductor, using what Stephanie could remember of his face from seeing him at the house in Turnberry Road, and what Jane Cashman could recall of him. The resulting likeness was so good that it scared Jane when she saw it. By 5th February, this likeness had appeared on the front page of the national press.

At the same time Tom Cook provoked a response from the kidnapper by making a public statement that he was half expecting a letter from him, boasting how successful he had been. Sure enough, the letter-happy correspondent wrote a three-page message to Tom Cook, sending copies of it to the two police forces, the press and television, and to Lynn Dart. The letter admitted the kidnapping of Stephanie, and apologised to her for it, but denied that there was any connection with the murder of Julie Dart or the British Rail extortion attempts. The letter carried the same punctuation and spelling errors as the earlier ones. Like the letters which followed Julie's kidnapping, the copy sent to the West Yorkshire police was addressed to

Michael Sams. (*Wolverhampton Express & Star*)

Millgate police station instead of Millgarth. Although the kidnapper was denying any connection, he managed to prove the opposite.

When Susan Oake saw the picture of the kidnapper in the newspaper it reminded her of her first husband, Michael Sams. She had married him when she was 18 and he was 20, but they had parted after 12 years when Sams became violent. She knew that since then he had married twice more; he now lived with his third wife Teena in Sutton on Trent, eight miles from Newark. When Susan read that the kidnapper wore a coat with a train motif, her suspicions increased a little more. Michael Sams had always been an avid trainspotter, fascinated by railways.

However, the description lacked one obvious clue: nowhere did it mention a limp. While serving a nine-month term in prison for car theft, Michael Sams had developed pains in his right leg. The prison authorities had ignored his complaints, putting him down as a whinger. When the pains turned out to be cancer, it was so far advanced that his leg had to be amputated above the knee. From that time he had bitterly resented all authorities: the police who had caught him in the first place, the magistrates who had sent him to prison for a first offence, the prison staff who had caused him to lose a leg.

The lack of any reference to the kidnapper having a handicap caused Susan Oake to put her suspicions out of her mind. Then, on 17th February, she saw and spoke to Michael again, at his father's funeral. He was driving an orange-red Metro. Three days later, Susan read in the press that a neighbour of the Slater family had seen a vermilion red Metro at the time that Stephanie had been dropped off at her home. The article said that on the *Crimewatch* programme on Thursday 20th February, the police would play a recording of the kidnapper's voice. Susan Oake was out when the programme came on, but her son videoed it for her. She watched the video when she came in at 11 pm, and immediately recognised her ex-husband's voice, which she had heard again recently at the funeral. When she heard Tom Cook mention that Stephanie had been kept in some kind of workshop, she immediately thought of the small power-tool business that Sams ran from his workshop at the Swan and Salmon yard in Newark. She tried to ring the *Crimewatch* number but all the lines were engaged. She rang her local police station who transferred

The police guard the entrance to the Swan and Salmon yard, in Castlegate, Newark. (*Newark Advertiser*)

her call to the Julie Dart incident room in Leeds. Susan told the Yorkshire police what she believed. Although Susan's was only one of many hundreds of phone calls received after *Crimewatch*, the detectives decided that it was one of the important ones, and two officers were dispatched to interview her. Everything she told them fitted except for the matter of the artificial leg. How could everyone have missed something like that? Nevertheless, Michael Sams moved to the top of the suspect list as far as the West Yorkshire police were concerned.

Four police officers visited Sams's home in Sutton on Trent the next morning. When Teena Sams told them that Michael was at work, they drove on to Newark and found his workshop in

Castlegate. As they entered, they heard his radio playing; it was still tuned in to Radio 2. Sams was arrested on a charge of murder and kidnapping and taken to Newark police station, where he confessed to the abduction of Stephanie Slater but denied that he had murdered Julie Dart. He continued in this denial through months of police questioning.

The trial of Michael Benniman Sams took place at Nottingham Crown Court in June 1993, before Mr Justice Judge. Having already pleaded guilty to the kidnapping of Stephanie Slater and to blackmailing Shipways, he now faced charges of murdering Julie Dart, attempting to blackmail the Leeds police over her release, and attempting to blackmail British Rail with a threat to derail a passenger train. Sams pleaded not guilty on each count.

In an opening address which lasted two and a half days, Mr Richard Wakerley QC, for the prosecution, told the court that Sams, a man with an IQ of 138, had plotted to commit the perfect crime. He wanted to prove to himself and to others that he could kidnap and blackmail successfully. He took pleasure in the execution of the plan, treating it as a game played against the police. He had kidnapped Julie Dart from the streets of Leeds in July 1991 and taken her to Newark where he held her prisoner. Despite all his meticulous planning, something went wrong. She may have seen Michael Sams's face or the place where she was being held, she may have resisted him in some way, so she had to die. Her body was placed in a wheelie-bin and was later dumped. Julie could not tell the court what had happened to her, although evidence of fibres and data from Sams's computer files would prove his guilt.

In January 1992, Sams had again kidnapped a young woman and held her for ransom. He succeeded in obtaining the money he demanded, but made mistakes and was caught. He had already pleaded guilty to charges of kidnapping, imprisoning and blackmail in that case. The victim, Stephanie Slater, would be giving evidence in court, and the details of the two cases were so overwhelmingly similar that the jury would have to conclude they were committed by the same man.

Witnesses gave evidence relating to Julie Dart's disappearance from Leeds, and a number of people reported that they had heard screams from the Castlegate area of Newark after midnight in mid-July in 1991. One witness said that, after the screams, she had seen Sams stagger out of his workshop, clutching his head and saying he had a migraine.

Then Stephanie Slater was called to the stand. She described her kidnapping to the court, and told how she had desperately tried to build up a rapport with Michael Sams, so that he would find it harder to kill her. She described the nightmare of her last day in the coffin-like box, when she was convinced that Sams would not return, and had contemplated suicide. In answer to cross-examination by David Milmo QC, the defence counsel, Stephanie said that, apart from the initial violent struggle, Sams had been gentle with her. Asked about Sams's limp, she replied that she thought he walked with a shuffle.

Dr Stephen Jones gave evidence about the cause of Julie Dart's death, and said the state of the body matched perfectly with the claims in the letters that it had been kept in a sealed wheelie-bin. Susan Oake gave details of recognising her ex-husband's voice when a tape was played on *Crimewatch*.

The main witness for the defence was Michael Sams. Much of his evidence concerned his mystery friend, the violent 'mate' he had told Stephanie Slater about. Sams said that this man had attempted to extort the money from British Rail and had killed Julie Dart. Faced with evidence that he had written the letters in the Julie Dart case, Sams replied that he had, but that it was at the dictation of the unnamed friend. Michael Sams continued to refuse to name the friend, claiming that if the police knew his identity they could decide to eliminate the man, in order to strengthen their present case. He said that he would provide the name after the trial was over.

Under cross-examination, Sams agreed that the rope and sheet found around Julie Dart's body were his, but denied that the mystery friend was in fact himself. He thought that the many similarities between the two cases were just coincidences. Asked about material found in the files of his computer which referred to the ransom of Julie Dart, Sams said that his friend must have put them there.

The jury of eight women and four men retired to consider their verdict, returning after three and a half hours to give a unanimous guilty verdict on all counts. The judge told Sams that he was an extremely dangerous and evil man. The letters written after the death of Julie Dart showed no qualms, no remorse, but instead callous arrogance and misplaced pride. He referred to the remarkable moral courage shown by Stephanie Slater, saying that she deserved the admiration of everyone in the court. The judge sentenced Sams to life imprisonment on each of four charges of murder, kidnapping and unlawful imprisonment, plus four sentences of ten years for the blackmail charges.

On the fourth day of his life sentence, Michael Sams confessed that he had murdered Julie Dart at 6 pm on Wednesday 10th July, keeping her body in a sealed wheelie-bin in his Newark workshop until 16th July. He had never blindfolded Julie; it hadn't mattered what she had seen as he had always intended she should die.

In 1995, Stephanie Slater, disturbed by stories that Michael Sams was boasting in prison that he and Stephanie had a special 'secret', decided to write her own story. In her book *Beyond Fear: My Will to Survive*, dedicated to the memory of Julie Dart, she revealed for the first time that Sams had raped her on the first night of her kidnap.

This revelation seemed to upset and anger Michael Sams. Never a man to let his grievances fade away, he held a female probation officer hostage in his prison cell inside Wakefield Prison. He captured Julie Flack, wife of the Bishop of Huntingdon, threatening her with a metal spike. After conducting his own defence at a trial at Durham Crown Court in 1997, he was found not guilty of attempting to murder Mrs Flack, but guilty of holding her hostage. A further eight years were added to his four life sentences. Sams explained that he was trying to focus public attention on his grievances against the prison authorities. First, they were preventing him from bringing a libel case against Stephanie Slater over her rape accusation, and secondly they were refusing to let him sell paintings he had done in prison.

Perhaps the final word about the cases of Julie Dart and Stephanie Slater should be that of Julie's mother. After hearing Stephanie's account of her captivity, Lynn Dart revealed one possible reason why Julie died whilst Stephanie survived. Julie had suffered from severe claustrophobia and would have fought like a wildcat rather than be put into the box inside the wheelie-bin. That, combined with her combative personality, could have led to her murder.

14

DEATH
OF A MILKMAN

The Murder of Philip Tizzard at Arnold
January 1992

Like most milkmen, Philip Tizzard made an early start to his working day. On Friday 24th January 1992 he left his house in Redhill Road, Arnold, at 3.30 am, intending to start his milkround in the St Ann's district of Nottingham. He drove his car to the end of the drive, then walked back to switch off the garage light and close the garage door. As he reached the garage, an attacker struck him a blow from behind, rendering him unconscious.

It was not long before his dead body was spotted by neighbours, lying half-in, half-out of the garage. They went to the house and informed Philip's wife, Maryse, and she phoned 999 for the police. They found that Mr Tizzard had been killed, having been attacked in the doorway of his garage.

The detective in charge of the murder inquiry, Detective Superintendent Stewart England, told a press conference that the 30 year old milkman had been subjected to a very violent attack. He quashed a rumour that armed officers were being used in the hunt for the killer, but said that the tactical response unit – which carries firearms in the boots of its cars – had been alerted after the discovery of the body, because the nature and severity of the injuries had initially led officers to believe that Philip Tizzard had been shot. They now knew that he had in fact been battered to death. The police had not yet discovered a motive for the crime, and they were searching for a heavy, blunt instrument. Mr Tizzard had been following his normal routine when he met his death, and it seemed as if the killer had been lying in wait for him. 'It would appear that there wasn't a tremendous struggle,' the detective continued, 'and that Mr Tizzard was struck numerous heavy blows to the head.'

Mrs Maryse Tizzard had been in the house with her four year old son at the time of the killing, but she was unaware of the incident until neighbours alerted her. Mrs Ivy Tizzard, the

MURDER
PHILIP TIZZARD

DID YOU KNOW PHILIP?

DO YOU HAVE ANY INFORMATION WHICH WOULD THROW ANY LIGHT ON THE REASON FOR THIS ATTACK?

Philip worked as a milkman with a delivery round in the St. Ann's area of Nottingham.

Shortly after 3.30 a.m. Friday 24th January 1992, he was about to leave his home at 14 Redhill Road, Arnold, Nottingham, when he was attacked. He died from severe head injuries.

We need your help in indentifying the killer.

Were you in the Arnold area in the early hours of Friday 24th January?

Did you see anyone or anything of a suspicious nature?

ANY PERSON WITH INFORMATION SHOULD CONTACT THE MURDER INCIDENT ROOM AT OXCLOSE LANE POLICE STATION ON NOTTM. 0602 670732.

The police appeal for witnesses.

grandmother of the murder victim, said that she only found out about the death when she heard about it on the radio, adding, 'It's a terrible way to find out that a member of your family has been killed.' She said that the family were devastated by what had happened, and described her 30 year old grandson as 'a fantastic lad who wouldn't hurt a fly'. John Tizzard of Primrose Street, Carlton, the dead man's uncle, said that Philip was 'a nice bloke, jovial and happy'.

Four days after the murder, the police issued a description of a man seen walking along High Street, Arnold, at 2.50 am on Friday, about 40 minutes before Philip Tizzard's body had been discovered. Based on a description provided by a lorry driver who had spotted him, he was described as white, about six feet tall with slim build, and aged about 30 to 35. He had light brown, collar-length hair combed back to reveal his forehead, and was wearing a light grey bomber jacket and grey trousers. The police now wished to interview this man.

Detectives said that they still had no idea why Tizzard should have been attacked. He and his wife and son had moved into the house the previous June. In October, Mr Tizzard had given up his previous employment as a gravedigger for Gedling Borough Council, and taken up the milkround franchise with the Greater Nottingham Co-op. The police were still seeking the murder weapon, now described as a blunt instrument with a flat edge, and certain to be bloodstained. It was thought that the killer's clothes were probably bloodstained too; these might have been discarded somewhere or might have been taken home to be washed. It was extremely important that any such bloodstained clothing was traced urgently. The police said that the response from the Nottingham public had been poor, and referred to meeting 'a wall of silence'.

By the end of February, a local organisation, the Community Action Trust, attempted to break through the wall by distributing posters in Arnold and St Ann's, offering a reward of £5,000 for information leading to the arrest of Philip Tizzard's killer. The police said that they had found no evidence of theft, robbery, burglary or any incident that would have involved Philip Tizzard in a dispute. The attack seemed to have been completely unprovoked and to have taken the victim totally by surprise. They thought it possible that something had happened in the past that might have led to the killing. They added that the man seen in the area 40 minutes before the attack had still not come forward.

On 4th April, the police made a breakthrough and three people – two men and a woman – were charged with the murder. The three, all from Arnold, were named as Adrian Lockley, 26, Paul Smith, 23, and Lisa Corah, 19. They appeared before a magistrates' court and were remanded in custody. Lisa Corah's application for bail was refused. The inclusion of Lisa Corah among the people charged was very significant: she was Maryse Tizzard's younger sister.

The trial – and it proved to be only the first trial – began on 23rd March 1993 at Nottingham Crown Court, before Mr Justice Judge. In his opening address, Mr Timothy Barnes QC, the prosecuting counsel, said that one of the accused – Lisa Corah, Tizzard's sister-in-law – claimed that Tizzard had raped and sexually abused her. She had told her friends of her hatred for Tizzard, adding that he had also betrayed her sister Maryse by having affairs with other women. The prosecution alleged that Lisa Corah had wanted Tizzard dead, and in Lockley and Smith she found two men who were prepared to do the deed for her. Adrian Lockley, Lisa's boyfriend, had become angry when he heard what Tizzard had allegedly done to her.

The three accused had held a murder dress rehearsal two days before the real killing. Three people had been observed outside Philip Tizzard's home late on 22nd January. One man was trying to get into the garage, another stood by the front door, and a woman was standing at the bottom of the drive. Two days later, Tizzard had been savagely killed and left in a pool of blood. Dr Stephen Jones, the Home Office pathologist, reported that Tizzard had been hit at least four times with a very heavy weapon, and that his ear was 'pulverised'. The murder weapon, a pickaxe handle, was found on a building site where Adrian Lockley worked. Forensic tests revealed traces of Tizzard's hair and blood on the instrument, as well as fibres from a jumper belonging to Lockley.

In a written statement, Mrs Maryse Tizzard said that her husband had set off for work at his usual time on the morning he was killed. After giving him his flask and workbag, she had gone back to bed before she was wakened by neighbours who had seen Philip's legs sticking out of the garage. She had dialled 999 first, then rung her sister Lisa, asking her to contact their father.

The prosecution alleged that minutes after Lisa Corah had received this telephone call, Adrian Lockley arrived at her house and handed her the murder weapon, which she hid behind the garden shed.

Amanda Carter, 19, gave evidence that her friend Lisa Corah had described the murder to her. The two of them had talked at various times on 7th March 1992, the day after Lisa, Adrian and Paul had been interviewed by the police. Giving her evidence in tears, Amanda recalled that Lisa had told her that Adrian and Paul had gone to Philip Tizzard's home, and Adrian had killed him, while Paul kept a lookout. Then Adrian had returned to Lisa's house and given her the murder weapon. Amanda told the court that Lisa had described having blood and hair all over her hands from the pickaxe handle. Amanda said that she had been shocked but she had not fully believed the story. She said that she had then confronted Adrian Lockley and asked him directly if he really had killed Philip Tizzard. He had gone quiet, then said, 'I don't know what you're talking about.' When she repeated her question, he had answered, 'I can't tell you, Mand, because you'll break under pressure.'

Alison Gadsby said that she had witnessed two men and a woman outside Tizzard's house late on the evening of Wednesday 22nd January.

Karen Richardson gave evidence that Adrian Lockley was with her at the time of the murder. She had been in bed when Lockley rang her in the early hours and asked if he could come round. He said he was phoning from his home, although she thought she could hear the sound of a car in the background. Five minutes later Lockley arrived at her house. He was wearing a black jacket and jeans; he had on dark grey trainers instead of his normal shoes. Karen said that she and Lockley had sex at about 2 am; then, to her surprise, her visitor got dressed and left. 'He seemed to be wound up,' she said. 'He was not his usual self.'

The court heard that Lisa Corah had bought Adrian Lockley a balaclava on the day before the killing, telling a work colleague that it was because Adrian was working out in the cold. Mrs Jean Martin, her supervisor, told the court that when Lisa returned to work five days after the killing, she was smiling and couldn't stop

A courtroom sketch of Adrian Lockley and Paul Smith. (*Nottingham Post*)

laughing to herself all day.

At this stage of the trial, Mr Peter Thornton QC, the defence counsel for Paul Smith, became ill. The judge discharged the jury 'with great reluctance', and the trial was abandoned on 29th March.

The retrial was held in Lincoln in May before Mr Justice Rougier. The new jury heard much of the evidence that had been presented at the abandoned trial in Nottingham. Timothy Barnes QC told the jury that the murder of Philip Tizzard had been planned for three months, and that the original idea had come from Lisa Corah.

The prosecution alleged that when the pickaxe handle was left with Lisa after the murder, she cut it into two pieces, putting them into a plastic bag. The bag was later returned to Lockley who buried it in the foundations of a house in Lincolnshire where he was working.

All three accused were arrested in early March. They were released after questioning, then rearrested when Lisa Corah confessed to a friend following a row with Lockley. After an argument with Adrian Lockley outside a party, Lisa told Amanda Carter, a barmaid at the Cross Keys pub in Arnold, 'He did it!' Lockley, on the other hand, told Amanda that he did not commit the murder, describing himself as 'a dumb boxer who was not clever enough'. (Lockley had been an amateur boxer, but had had to quit because he could not control his temper in the ring.)

Forensic scientist Duncan McCurdy told the court that blood found on the pickaxe handle was of the same group as Tizzard's. A DNA test also matched. The handle had been recovered from a house in Fellingham.

Lisa Corah said that Tizzard had forced her to have sex with him when they were on a family holiday in Corfu. She was then 14 years old and a virgin. She didn't tell anyone at the time because she was ashamed. Her brother-in-law had raped her again in 1989 on the day her sister Maryse was giving birth. 'It was not with my consent,' she sobbed, 'and it was more than once. I hated him after that. I wanted to keep it from my sister – I loved her very much.' When she had mentioned these events to Adrian Lockley, he had become angry and threatened to break Tizzard's neck. In the early hours of the day Tizzard died, Lisa said that she was woken up by someone shouting her name from the back garden. It was Adrian and he had Paul Smith with him. 'I asked them what they wanted and Adrian said, "He's dead!" I asked who and he said "Tizzard".' Lisa told the jury that she had refused Lockley's offer to marry her, but added that she did not go to the police because she was frightened of losing him. She said that on the day after the killing, Lockley was talking to her in the bedroom of her home, and told her that he had done it for her and that he loved her.

At this stage, two members of the jury were taken ill and it seemed as if this second trial could meet the same fate as the first. However, the judge ordered a doctor to be summoned. He treated the jurors and the trial continued.

On 18th May, the jury retired to consider their verdict. When they returned, they found Adrian Lockley guilty of murder, and Lisa Corah guilty of aiding and abetting the murder. Paul Smith, who like Lockley had chosen not to give evidence at the trial, was cleared of any crime. Sentencing both Lockley and Corah to life imprisonment, Mr Justice Rougier said, 'This was an appalling crime which must have sickened every decent person who has heard the details.' Addressing Lisa Corah, he continued, 'I accept that in the past Tizzard violated you and you had cause to hate him. I can see no other reason for you to feel how you did, but that was in the past. You have now brought down your lover, destroyed yourself, your brother-in-law and your family.'

Two years later, in May 1995, the Court of Appeal heard that new evidence rendered the conviction of Lisa Corah unsafe and unsatisfactory. Her counsel, Ben Emerson, said that there were three grounds for appeal. First, he claimed that trial judge Mr Justice Rougier had wrongly admitted a transcript of evidence given by a witness at the earlier trial. Secondly, in his summing up the judge had failed to clear up identification evidence. Thirdly, there was much material which rendered the conviction unsafe. The Court of Appeal accepted the argument, and quashed Lisa Corah's conviction, ordering that she should face a new trial. An appeal on behalf of Adrian Lockley was turned down.

The retrial of Lisa Corah took place at Nottingham Crown Court before Mr Justice Garland, beginning on 31st October. Charles Wide QC, for the prosecution, told the jury that there was no dispute that Adrian Lockley killed Tizzard as he was leaving his home to go to work in the early hours of Friday 24th January 1992. He had hit the victim many times with a pickaxe handle, causing fatal head injuries. The prosecution claimed that Lisa Corah was part of a reconnaissance held two nights earlier, when she had been seen with two men outside Tizzard's house. Corah had told people that Tizzard had raped her and she believed he had been unkind and unfaithful to his wife, her sister Maryse. Lisa Corah had confessed to her best friend, Amanda Carter, that she had been given the murder weapon after the killing, and had hidden it. She told the same friend that the murder had been planned for three months.

Cross-examined by Helena Kennedy QC, for the defence, Amanda Carter agreed that Lisa had said that she had been told about the plan to attack Tizzard after the killing had taken place.

Julie Freestone was called by the prosecution, and gave evidence that she had shared a detention cell at the city's Guildhall Court with Lisa Corah in April 1992. She claimed that Lisa had told her that she was up for murder, and that when her boyfriend had 'done' her brother-in-law, she had been there, sitting in a car. Under cross-examination by the defence, Julie Freestone admitted that she had been a professional thief and a prostitute, but denied that she was an inveterate liar who had it in for Lisa Corah because she believed she should have stood by Lockley.

Lisa Corah gave evidence that being raped by Philip Tizzard had affected her sexual relationship with Adrian Lockley, who was very possessive and jealous. She now felt that the murder was all her fault, and would never have happened if she hadn't told Adrian how her brother-in-law had raped her. She said that she had thought of going to the police and telling them what she knew, but she thought her family would disown her, and she also felt a sort of loyalty to Adrian. She said that Adrian had been her first serious boyfriend but she had problems with her sex life because the rapes had made her feel dirty. When she had finally told Adrian what the problem was, he had become angry and upset. Her life had become a nightmare after Adrian had brought the murder weapon to her home and told her Philip Tizzard was dead.

Ernest and Mary Corah told the court that their daughter Lisa had been at home on the night of the murder, watching television in her room with Adrian Lockley. Adrian had left at about midnight.

Witness Alison Gadsby said that she had picked out Lisa Corah on a police identification parade as the woman she had seen outside Tizzard's house. Rene Corah, Lisa's brother, told the jury that he thought the identification parade was unprofessional; Lisa had looked tired and drawn while the others were all well dressed and well groomed. Some of the girls had long dark hair, in contrast to Lisa's short fair hair. When he had complained to the police at the time, he had been told, 'Don't be a prat.'

Helena Kennedy addressed the jury, telling them that at the heart of the case was a horrible violation of an adolescent girl by a man she had thought of as her brother. This had had terrible reverberations and outcomes – but that didn't make Lisa Corah a murderer. Lisa's revelations to Lockley about what her brother-in-law had done to her had awful consequences, but if there had been a plan to kill Mr Tizzard, it certainly did not include Lisa Corah. It was more likely that the attack on Mr Tizzard was not planned but was a bid to teach him a lesson that went horribly wrong.

Nine days after the trial began, the jury of eight men and four women retired for two hours. When they returned they announced a unanimous verdict of not guilty, and Lisa Corah left the court a free woman.

15

SATANISM v.
WITCHCRAFT

The Murder of Christopher Rogers in Carlton
February 1993

Responding to a phone call, Nottingham police officers went to an address in Standhill Road, Carlton, in the early hours of Sunday 21st February 1993. There they found the body of Christopher Rogers, a Manchester City councillor and vice-chairman of Manchester Education Committee. Two other men were present, one of whom said to the officers, 'There's no problem. I have killed him. I said I would do it and I have done it.' Told that he was being arrested on suspicion of murder, the man, Colin Henry, replied, 'Suspicion? There is no suspicion about it. I have killed him.'

An inquest into the death of Councillor Rogers was opened on 24th February, and the coroner, Mr Peter Jenkin-Jones, heard that the body had been identified by Nicholas McGregor, who lived at the same address as Christopher Rogers in Levershulme, Manchester, and who had known him for over 20 years. A preliminary post-mortem report showed that the cause of death was shock and haemorrhage due to stab injuries to the chest. The inquest was then adjourned, pending criminal proceedings.

The trial of Colin Henry, a 37 year old joiner, took place a year later at Nottingham Crown Court, before Mr Justice Gage. The prosecuting counsel, Peter Joyce QC, told the court that on 21st February 1993, Henry had telephoned Carlton police station at 2.40 am and said that he had just killed someone with a six-inch knife. When asked why, he had replied, 'He called me stupid.' Mr Joyce said that Colin Henry lived in Standhill Road with his partner, Paul Simmonds, and the two of them had made the

120

acquaintance of Christopher Rogers. They had met occasionally in Nottingham and Manchester, and had arranged a meeting in February 1993. After Councillor Rogers had attended a seminar in Nottingham, Paul Simmonds met him in a restaurant, and took him back to his house.

Later that evening, a heated argument about the occult had developed between Colin Henry and Christopher Rogers, and Rogers was asked to leave. However, it was eventually agreed that Rogers could sleep on the sofa. The prosecution told the court that the argument may well have been about the relative merits of satanism and witchcraft.

At about 1 am, Paul Simmonds and Colin Henry went upstairs to bed. Both had difficulty in sleeping, and sometime later, Colin got up to make a cup of tea. After he had gone downstairs, Paul heard the door of the lounge open and Colin shout, 'You won't ever call me stupid again', in a loud voice. Paul saw Colin Henry at the foot of the stairs, saying, 'I have killed him. I had better call the police.' The prosecution alleged that at the police station, Henry had told officers, 'I gave him six inches of solid steel and now all my aggression is gone.' Counsel then told the jury that it was likely that they would hear a suggestion that Colin Henry acted under provocation, and they would therefore have to consider whether Henry was suffering from diminished responsibility.

Dr Stephen Jones, the Home Office pathologist, told the court that the distribution of injuries on the dead man's body was the most bizarre he had ever seen. There were two stab wounds in Rogers's chest, both of them potentially fatal, but there were other marks on the nipples, back and buttocks that were typical of the application of pain to derive pleasure. 'I cannot exclude the possibility of the injuries being inflicted by a whip,' he said.

Paul Simmonds, Colin Henry's partner, told the court that he had met Christopher Rogers through a contact magazine in 1987. Rogers had come to stay at their home on 20th February, and, after watching television, he said that he had brought some videos with him. Rogers changed into silky transvestite-type clothing and they had watched two pornographic, sado-masochistic videos. Simmonds said that during a heated argument, Rogers had called Colin Henry stupid, and was asked to leave. Simmonds said that he had tried to calm the situation down, and it was eventually agreed that Christopher Rogers could stay the night on a settee in the lounge.

He said that after Colin had gone downstairs to make a cup of tea, he had heard him shout aggressively, 'You won't call me stupid again.' The next thing he heard was Colin saying, 'I'm sorry Paul, but I've killed him.'

Cross-examined by Conrad Seagroat QC, for the defence, Paul Simmonds agreed that he had once had a sexual encounter with Mr Rogers and another man in the cellar of Rogers's Manchester home. He described the cellar as being dungeon-like, and equipped with sado-masochistic devices. Simmonds said that Councillor Rogers's interest in the occult had frightened him.

At the request of the defence counsel, the jury then watched a 15-minute extract from a sado-masochistic video called *Dungeons of Europe*. They were told that the video was owned by Christopher Rogers and was one of the two videos that were played on the night of his death. Before watching, Mr Justice Gage warned the jury that its contents were extremely distasteful and distressing.

Continuing his evidence under cross-examination, Paul Simmonds said that it was obvious during the evening that Christopher Rogers was trying to psychoanalyse Colin Henry. He started to 'rubbish' Henry's belief in witchcraft. Simmonds said that Rogers had an overwhelming personality that was hypnotic.

Colin Henry, a twice-married carpenter and joiner, told the court that he was not happy when his partner had invited Rogers to stay at their home. He said that Rogers was constantly belittling his faith in Celtic witchcraft and trying to convert him to satanism. He told Rogers to go and stay the night at a hotel, but later he agreed that he could stay. He said that he was unable to sleep because he kept thinking of how Rogers had 'slagged off' his beliefs. On the way to the kitchen to make a cup of tea, he asked Rogers if he wanted one, but he declined. 'After that, it's just little bits of memory,' Colin Henry said. He remembered being in the kitchen one minute, and the next he was standing in the front room with a knife in his hand. Christopher Rogers was standing in front of him. 'He moved and I moved with him,' said Henry. 'The next thing he's falling through the doors and I'm down beside him and I've got a knife in my hand and he's laid on the floor, dead. I felt like What-have-I-done? I felt like crying. I know

I screamed something. I know I closed his eyelids and then thought I had better phone the police.'

Nottingham consultant psychiatrist Dr David Gill told the jury that he thought that Rogers had subjected Colin Henry to severe psychological pressure, and that had led to conflict. This began because Henry did not want Rogers in the house that night. Next, there was a small incident when Rogers demanded a change of television programme, and then for three hours Rogers took centre stage. Wittingly or unwittingly, he subjected Colin Henry as a captive audience to a series of torments. 'He cross-dressed in women's clothes, he repeatedly sexually stimulated himself, and he put on pornographic videos of sado-masochistic activities. He taunted Colin Henry about what part of his body he would like to have cut off, and despite Henry's protests, he continued with this taunt.' Dr Gill said that Christopher Rogers had boasted to Henry of his involvement in the abduction, torture and death of four or five young men. Finally he extolled the merits of Lucifer and satanism and, as Henry saw it, he attempted to convert him to his own perverted beliefs.

Dr Gill said that he interviewed Colin Henry for three and a half hours. He said that Henry told him that he now felt as if a great big weight had been lifted from his shoulders, like lead coming off him. 'He said that it was as if a terrible threat had been lifted from the world, and now happiness was present where there just used to be darkness,' Dr Gill continued. Henry had told him that it was nice to see the police officers when they came to the house in response to his call. They were human beings, whereas he'd been in the presence of Christopher Rogers, who wasn't human. Colin Henry was repelled by Christopher Rogers, who he believed had 'mental powers to manipulate him'. After his arrest, Henry told Dr Gill he had picked up a sheath knife and said to Rogers, 'So I am stupid, am I?' Twice when Rogers had come towards him, he had struck him with the knife, then shouted, 'You are not going to call me stupid any more.'

Consultant forensic psychiatrist Dr Anthony Maden told the court that he believed that Colin Henry had received psychological injury by being provoked by Christopher Rogers, and that his mental responsibility was very substantially impaired at the time of the alleged offence. Dr Maden said that some of the things that Henry told him during four and a half hours of interviews were bordering on delusions. The defendant believed Christopher Rogers was an evil man who had almost mystical powers, and had been trained by an international band of satanists in techniques for breaking down other people. Dr Maden said that, in his opinion, Colin Henry suffered from a personality disorder of a paranoid nature. He had suffered a severe psychological trauma during the evening before the killing, and it had all become too much for him. He had had a breakdown, a brief psychotic reaction.

Summing up, the defence counsel Conrad Seagroat told the jury that the case was not about the normal, the supernormal or the paranormal, but the abnormal. It was not about satanism and sado-masochism on the one hand and witchcraft, folklore and pagan ritual on the other. It was about the mental conflict between two men on that particular night. Colin Henry felt subject to the power of evil and although he felt he had done a service in removing that source of evil, the killing was not done deliberately in the sense that it was a premeditated or a calculated act. He called on the jury to return a verdict of manslaughter, not murder, asking them, 'Can you doubt that Colin Henry was subjected to some form of psychological assault that night?' There was overwhelming evidence of the abnormality of Henry's mind, he continued, and that evidence was all one way, with nothing at all to contradict it.

For the prosecution, Peter Joyce said that the murder had been a cold and calculated killing of revenge, with Henry boasting about what he had done. 'This was a very cold, petulant act for being called stupid, and it's as cheap and nasty as that,' he concluded.

The jury of 11 men and one woman retired to consider their verdict. After deliberating for four and a half hours, they brought in a unanimous verdict of murder. Colin Henry stood with his head bowed as Mr Justice Gage told him, 'On the evidence in this court it seems pretty clear that Mr Rogers had been behaving in a particularly obnoxious and unpleasant way, but that does not in any way justify this killing. No one is entitled to act as you have done.' Henry received a life sentence for the murder.

After the trial, Paul Simmonds stated that he and Colin Henry had only been interested in natural magic: worship of the seasons, herbal medicine, and ancient Celtic rituals and beliefs.

Detective Constable John Parlatt of Nottinghamshire CID stated, 'This is a tragic matter where a number of lives have been affected by the death of one man. I would like the gay community in Nottingham to know that we investigated things in an impartial way.'

INDEX